W9-CXZ-929

DONE BY NOON ®

How To Achieve More By Noon Than Other Entrepreneurs In A Full Day

DAVE RUEL

MuscleMind Media Inc.
MARKETING & PUBLISHING

DONE BY NOON®
How To Achieve More By Noon Than Other Entrepreneurs In A Full Day

ISBN: 978-0-9959977-7-6

DONE BY
NOON®

Praises

"Almost every entrepreneur has felt overwhelmed and burned out at some point in their journey. And with grind and hustle being the message of the day that contributes to this burnout, there is no better person than Dave to remedy the situation because of his ability to understand what ALL entrepreneurs go through, while helping them get more clarity and structure in their business so they can once again enjoy business and life. Dave shares a powerful message that all entrepreneurs need to hear."

Yuri Elkaim,
Entrepreneur and New-York Times Best-Selling Author

"I've tried dozens of organizational systems in the past, but most of them have fallen short... Each time I used them, they all seemed to be either lacking what I truly needed as a busy professional, or they were too hard to implement. I'm now in perfect control of my quarterly, weekly, and daily planning."

Dr. Stephen Cabral,
ND & Founder Cabral Wellness Institute

"Dave's methods have impacted our businesses so much in such a short amount of time… However, it all boils down to this: what we implemented took our business from behind-the-scenes chaos that felt messy, reactive, and stressful to run, to one that is simplified, streamlined, and ENJOYABLE again. We can't thank you enough Dave for what you've created with this system. It's changed the way we run our business AND our team!"

Jill Stanton,
Online Entrepreneur, ScrewTheNineToFive.com

"… made for my brain as an entrepreneur. It keeps me focused on the outcome and impact I am looking to achieve."

Dr. Meghan Walker,
ND, Entrepologist

"As a busy father and entrepreneur, I am always trying to optimize my daily routine and the systems in my business to allow me to do the things I love. If you don't know Dave, he is a Jedi Master of creating systems and leveraging your strengths. And because of that, he instantly taught me how to leverage my skills to get the most out of my time and in turn has helped make me more productive and effective as a leader, content creator, and businessman. As a classic small business owner and procrastinator, I used to have a tendency to get overwhelmed with what I want to accomplish as far as growth and big goals are concerned. What you'll find in this book has helped me clarify my vision and big goals and create a roadmap of smaller, bite-sized tasks to allow me to achieve the life and business of my dreams. Now, I'm able to work 5 hours per day and enjoy more time being present with my wife and five kids without having my mind wandering over to business issues any more."

Chris Lopez,
Online Entrepreneur

Contents

Introduction

As he handed me a fresh cup of coffee, he told me he was earning six figures a year from his fitness blog.

That was the first time I met one in person. It was like seeing a unicorn. Everyone talks about them, but no one has ever seen one. Except that this time it was real! A lifestyle entrepreneur in the flesh!

I always pictured myself waking up without the help of an alarm clock, enjoying breakfast with my family without having to rush, and working on things that I was genuinely passionate about without feeling under pressure. We're sold an image of a lifestyle-driven entrepreneur who works from his laptop on the beach, and I wanted to live that life. You probably wanted the same thing.

In my early 20's, I became obsessed with fitness. That obsession led me to compete as a physique athlete. That's when I met a man who would become a great friend and my first mentor: Lee Hayward.

While traveling to his hometown for a show we were both competing in, Lee invited me to stay at his house. Lee and I knew each other from the regional circuit, but I didn't know what he was doing for a living.

I'll always remember a conversation we had one morning. We were standing in his kitchen, cooking breakfast.

He said, "This morning, I have a few things to do, and I have to reply to a few emails, I should be done by noon. We can hit the gym early in the afternoon, and I was thinking about catching a movie at the theatre later, is that OK with you?"

It was a Thursday morning.

As I didn't know what he was doing for a living, I automatically assumed Lee was off work, just like I was. I said, "It feels good to be on vacation, right? I wish every day could be like this."

"Oh, it's a pretty typical day here," he replied.

"Mmm… What do you mean?"

"My work is pretty much always completed by noon."

"What is it that you do exactly?"

Lee explained that he was making a full time living from his bodybuilding blog that he'd been running since 1999. He went on to tell me he was making six figures every year selling bodybuilding and fitness information, programs, and products online. His wife Trish had also recently quit her day job to work with him.

At that exact moment, my life changed forever.

My fellow competitor had the freedom to do *whatever* he wanted, *whenever* he wanted, *however* he wanted.

Lee was living a life I thought was some kind of utopic vision...

I just couldn't believe it! Someone was actually living the exact kind of life I had always dreamed of. More importantly, he was doing it in complete alignment with our shared passion.

From there, I traded my passion for fitness for an obsession with business. Within just seven years, I developed an online health and fitness mini-empire. I sold over 100,000 health and fitness books published in multiple languages, started and ran a publishing and digital marketing agency, and grew a natural supplements company from zero to $3.2 million in annual sales.

By entrepreneurial standards, I was a success story. But in reality, I had become enslaved by my business, working up to 80 hours a week. It was far from what I'd envisioned when I started my business.

As you probably know, as glamorous as entrepreneurship looks from the outside, the reality is a different story.

Just like me, you probably thought that being your own boss would be different, right?

The truth is that you're probably reading this book because the hopes and expectations you had for your business haven't panned out. If so, you're not alone. This is an all too familiar story for most entrepreneurs.

I think most entrepreneurs can easily relate to this: You were tired of working for someone else, you wanted to be able to make your own schedule, be paid to do what you love and spend more time with your loved ones; you wanted to be free to live life on your own terms and do something meaningful at the same time. That's why you became an entrepreneur.

But what you didn't anticipate was what came with entrepreneurship.

You got sucked into the dark side of entrepreneurship, always chasing "more," losing sight of the very reasons why you became an entrepreneur in the first place. As time went on, you developed tunnel vision and ended up forgetting about the most important things.

Entrepreneurship isn't easy, and no one prepares you for that. Most of us eventually end up losing control of our workload. We end up drowning in a sea of tasks that keep pushing us down. We're unable to focus on what will really make an impact on our business. Also, the lack of boundaries between our life and business takes a toll on our health and family life. We can't stop thinking about work, and it feels like our business is taking over our entire existence.

We know that we're capable of much more, but all we do is put out fires so we can stay alive.

It's as though you're riding a dragon. While others think you're brave and awesome, you're thinking "How the hell did I end up on a dragon, and how do I keep from getting eaten?" while what you genuinely want is to be there waiting for your kids when they get out of the school bus so you can make them a snack.

The problem with today's entrepreneurial culture is that it promotes extreme work behaviors, with complete disregard to human needs or individual capacities. It glorifies the "hustle" and guilts those who want to live more. It's a culture that says you're less of a person because you want to *live* rather than just exist.

That's what happened to me.

You see, when I started my entrepreneurial journey, I realized that fitness and business were not that different. I discovered that the skills required to be a performant athlete were strangely similar to those needed to become a productive and performant entrepreneur.

The structure I had gained from my years as a physique athlete became my ultimate advantage that quickly earned me success

Unfortunately, I got sucked into this world of excess. I ended up riding a 3-headed dragon that would have consumed me entirely if I hadn't made some critical changes.

I realized that to fulfill my mission through entrepreneurship, I needed to change the way I lead my business, starting with myself. I needed to create a structure that still allowed me to perform and be productive, that gave me the space I wanted and also offered sustainability, respecting the fact that entrepreneurship is a long-term game of patience and consistency.

This is how the Effic company was born and why this book got written: to help entrepreneurs and small businesses increase productivity and performance by employing smarter, simpler, and sustainable working methods and systems while protecting their freedom.

We are now renowned internationally, teaching our methodology, systems, and frameworks around the world via our network of certified professionals. We've helped thousands of entrepreneurs from dozens of different countries.

The great news is that we're here together today. And here's some even better news: you are in control. Things might look chaotic now, but if you want your life and business to be back on track, there is a new path you can take. It starts today. You'll discover a new way of operating a company that is aligned with what you want. You'll learn how to perform sustainably without sacrificing what's important while enjoying fulfilling growth in both your personal and professional life.

I will show you how to take control of your workload, schedule, and entrepreneurial life by implementing cutting-edge, proven techniques that free up your time, lower your stress, and multiply your productivity without sacrificing yourself or your family.

Here's what you can expect to learn and implement with this book:

- How to finish what you used to do in 40+ hours per week in half the time.

- How to double your productivity by focusing on two daily tasks while keeping everything else on controlled autopilot.

- Simple, proven, high-performance routines and rituals.

- A system for swatting away external distractions and managing your overflow of ideas.

- The complete framework that will allow you to optimally manage your time, energy, and attention to ensure you'll perform at work and win at your personal life.

- How to prioritize tasks to create the space in your schedule for what really matters.

- ·The fireproof system where you never have to put out fires, deal with non-stop emergencies, or handle never-ending to-do lists.

But before you get too excited, I want to make something clear: if you're looking for shortcuts or hacks, this book is not for you.

This book isn't some kind of magic bullet that will instantly transport you to a hammock between two palm trees while money magically flies into your bank account. This is a fantasy, and I think we all know it.

But if your goal is to build a business that works *for* you instead of enslaving you, then this is the right book for you.

These strategies will transform how you operate, regardless of your ambitions or how many hours you want to work. It presents a new paradigm for entrepreneurs to lead themselves and their businesses sustainably.

So, if you're ready to achieve more by noon than others in a full day, let's get started.

Part 1:

We, entrepreneurs

The 5 Truths About Life &
Business As Entrepreneurs

I never made a conscious decision to become an "entrepreneur." In fact—and this is something you might have experienced too—I never realized I was an entrepreneur until someone used the word to describe me. Now, that was before the word "entrepreneur" was cool, and everybody wanted to be one. It seems that in today's world, everyone calls themselves an entrepreneur before they accomplish anything, even if the label doesn't fit what they do or who they are.

What makes entrepreneurs so special is that they are passionate about pursuing their dreams. They are a unique breed of people. The world's most successful entrepreneurs aren't the ones who impulsively quit their jobs to chase a get-rich-quick idea. Entrepreneurs are interested in other things besides making money. They are the ones with a creative mindset that allows them to solve the world's problems.

We have a unique mix of ingenuity, resilience, and a little bit of craziness that allows us to come up with big visions, identify opportunities, and be comfortable with uncertainty.

At the same time, we are all individuals. Each of us starts a business in different circumstances and in a unique context. For example, some of us are single, and others have families. We also have different levels of ambition. Some entrepreneurs want to build massive empires, but others are more attracted to simpler businesses.

We all start out with our own unique set of life and business experiences. Usually, we start a business based around a talent or skill that we've honed over time, and it shapes the work we do in years to come. We also all have different values and principles, and these underpin the way we operate our businesses and live our lives. For example, some of us value family and relationships above everything else. If that applies to you, you will run your business in a way that allows you to spend as much quality time as you can with your loved ones.

Yet despite our differences, we share similar patterns when it comes to the way we operate.

Every entrepreneur is a human being looking for fulfillment, meaning, and purpose. Entrepreneurs want to leave their mark on the world while living in alignment with their core values and personal vision. They aren't content to build someone else's dreams. They are proactive and strive to live an authentic life.

Before we dive more in-depth, I want to establish five truths about life and business as an entrepreneur. Some might already be familiar, whereas others will be new to you. But no matter what, you'll face these truths along your entrepreneurial journey.

Truth#1: All Entrepreneurs Want Freedom

The engine that drives entrepreneurship is pretty simple and is something each and every one of us cherishes: the desire for FREEDOM. It's what we all seek when we start a business. We all start from a different place, but ultimately, we all want the same thing.

► The 3 Entrepreneurial Freedoms

There are three types of freedom in entrepreneurship:

1.**Time Freedom:** We want to do things **whenever** we want, without having to report to anyone. As entrepreneurs, if we don't want to work a traditional 9-5, we don't have to.

2. **Creative Freedom:** We want to work on **whatever** we want. We want to take on projects that make us go "Hell yeah!" without having to do things we hate. As entrepreneurs, we have very creative minds. Starting a business lets us fulfill our desire to create something and make an impact.

3. Financial Freedom: We want to own a business that generates enough revenue to support our lifestyle.

As you develop as an entrepreneur, each of these freedoms may become more or less important depending on your context, but it always comes back to these three components.

► Freedom Requires Juggling Skills

Remember how you felt when you decided to become an entrepreneur? You were tired of working for someone else, you craved the liberty to live by your own schedule, you wanted to make a living from your passion or skills, and you wanted to spend more time with your loved ones.

Financial freedom is probably the #1 most sought-after milestone for everyone making the jump into entrepreneurship. We know we have a solution in our hands that can benefit others and that they'll pay for it. We monetize our creative freedom through our business. You might think that when you have enough money, you'll be able to buy more time. After realizing you can't actually buy more time, you'll go on a quest to reclaim it. In fact, if you're at this stage in your journey, that's probably why you're reading this.

You'll soon realize that your lack of time freedom is limiting your ability to pursue more creative freedom, which in turn supports greater self-expression.

When you've achieved financial freedom, you'll also realize that money isn't what fulfills you as an entrepreneur. If freedom is the engine behind entrepreneurship, you'll soon see money as a fuel that drives you towards greater happiness and purpose.

Because they work in complex but synergic ways, you'll have to learn how to continually juggle these three freedoms throughout your journey as an entrepreneur.

► The Engine's Performance Depends On You

If freedom is an engine where money is fuel, your creativity becomes the spark plug, the fire that ignites the fuel and turns it into power, while time is the throttle.

The great news is that you operate that throttle. Your driving behavior will dictate how much freedom you'll have. Keep this metaphor in mind, as it will be vital in understanding how you should measure your performance. Spoiler alert: more power doesn't mean better performance.

Truth #2: Entrepreneurs Love To Work

I always ask aspiring entrepreneurs this question: "Why do you want to start a business?"

Typically, they tell me, "I want to make money so I can quit my job and never have to work for someone else ever again!"

I then ask them a follow-up question: "If you had so much money that you'd never have to work again, would you stop working?" This question separates entrepreneurs from those who merely think they want to start a business.

As entrepreneurs, we don't see retirement in our future. We think it's a weird concept. For us, work is a meaningful and productive life activity. It's not just about getting paid and making money. This is a limited view of what "work" means.

Work gives us a sense of satisfaction. It involves making something, serving someone, and providing something of value to individuals or your community. I believe that by nature, entrepreneurs need and desire productive activity.

Let's be honest: You picked up this book because something about the way you work right now isn't working for you. You didn't pick it up because you're lazy, but because you wanted to reconnect with your freedom. You want to create the best possible conditions that empower you to do meaningful work.

In the early stages of your entrepreneurial journey, the truth is that you'll be focused on earning enough money to support your lifestyle. Then, once you've achieved financial freedom, you can start enjoying freedom of time and freedom of creation.

All entrepreneurs agree that there is nothing like the satisfaction that comes with growing a successful, impactful business that lets us use our skills and talents. I think of us, entrepreneurs, as practical artists. We draw on our unique perspective and experience to offer real solutions to existing problems. There is true beauty and artistry in producing great work that is in alignment with our calling. Connecting with the needs of the world by using our natural skills, acquired mastery, interests, and passion is a beautiful thing.

Even when the work gets hard, we love it. In the same way that muscle soreness during or after a training session shows we are making progress, we see discomfort as a positive sign of growth in our business. As long as you know what you're doing and what you want to achieve, the pain is an indication that something is working.

Entrepreneurs don't work for the sake of it. We work because it makes us a greater version of ourselves. It's an expression of our identity. When you're in a mindset that values outstanding, high-impact work, you don't seek the easy path. Instead, you seek the "right" path. In this book, we emphasize "right," not "less" or "more."

Work lets us fulfill our creative side. However, this is only possible when we work under the right conditions, and when we work on the right things. If you spend your days fighting against an unmanageable workload and putting out fires, you won't be able to reach your potential or make an impact. If this sounds familiar, you're suffering from the symptoms of drift. It happens to everyone at some point. In the next section, we'll look at why and how this happens.

Truth #3: Drift Happens

Entrepreneurs love to work, but…

You knew this was coming.

When we start a business, we usually base it around something that we do well. Typically, it's something that comes naturally to us and for which we developed a passion.

Having established your reputation as an expert in your field, you become an entrepreneur. Everything begins to click into place. But then, often slowly at first, you get busier and busier. You start doing tasks that you did not envision doing when you started out. This is what we call drift. Little by little, we drift away from what made us great in the first place. This can happen so slowly that we don't even realize we're doing it.

Drifting comes at a cost.

Unfortunately, we often fail to see that cost because we try to rationalize it. We attempt to justify spending time on tasks that aren't in our area of expertise. We convince ourselves that doing everything yourself is necessary for the growth of your business. We tell ourselves things like: *"I'm saving quite a bit of money by doing this myself"* or *"I don't have time to explain this to someone else."* We're usually really good at this.

But there's a significant financial and energetic cost to operating your business in this way. Not only will you miss out on the chance to maximize your profits, but you will also waste precious energy.

Consider this: It takes much more energy, brainpower, and time to do something when you don't have a natural aptitude for it. It's more productive to use your finite resources on tasks you have a talent for.

► The 5 Zones Of Activity

Take a look at the map below. It shows the various zones we find ourselves in as we run our business.

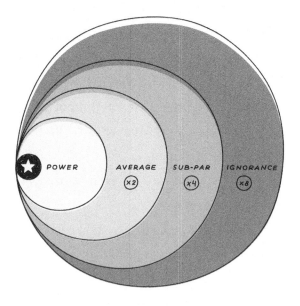

Your Superpower

At the far left is your superpower. This is your top area of expertise, your true magic. This is the "thing" we do better than 99%

of other people. This is the one thing that sets you apart from the competition and why other people come to you for advice because you are exceptional in this area. If you lost everything and could only use one skill to rebuild, that'd be this one!

Power Zone

The power zone consists of things you do better than most people. These are natural abilities or skills you were born with. You didn't have to learn how to be good at them. Through optimization, you've discovered how to perform them to a high standard. These are activities that you do with enthusiasm, and you rarely get tired or bored of doing them.

Your success depends on how much time you spend using your superpower and the power zone around it. Unfortunately, we more than often drift into these zones:

Average Zone

In the average zone lies the type of tasks that you don't mind doing, but aren't particularly skilled at. You'd prefer to have them done by someone else, but you are neither great nor bad at them. Many of the tasks involved in running your business fit into this zone.

Subpar Zone

These are tasks you're not great at, yet you still do them because you think it's the "price you pay to be in business." But you're not good at these tasks, and it takes you a lot of energy to perform them.

Ignorance Zone

This zone is to be avoided. In this zone, you have no idea what you are doing. Unfortunately, a lot of entrepreneurs venture into the ignorance zone anyway, trying to do these tasks because they think taking a DIY approach will save them money.

You have to consider this issue from both a financial and energetic perspective. Look at the chart above. Each area outside your power zone contains a financial and energetic coefficient. Every task you do outside of it carries a financial and energetical cost. It doubles every time you venture into the next zone. We call this the drifting coefficient.

► The Drifting Cost Exercise

This is a great little exercise you can use yourself and with your clients if you're a coach. It's called the Drifting Cost exercise, and it works by calculating work-time value.

THE DRIFTING COST

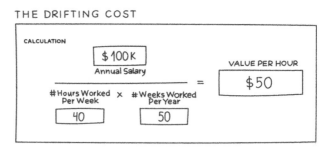

All you need to do is enter the right figures and run a simple calculation, as shown on the worksheet above.

1. Begin by entering your annual salary. For the sake of this exercise, let's say it's $100,000.

2. Next, you need to take into account the number of hours you work per week. This varies significantly between entrepreneurs. Here, we're going to assume an average of 40 hours a week.

3. Write down the number of weeks you worked last year. In this case, let's assume that you worked for 50 weeks (and that you took two weeks of vacation time).

   Note: You must use figures from the last 12 months when entering your annual salary. This figure must represent your take-home pay—the money that lands in your bank account.

   You must use this number if you want to learn how much money you are generating from your business efforts. If you are not making enough money, it means you are not in a good financial position. You may need to examine your business model rather than just focus on how to optimize your time.

4. Multiply your average weekly working hours by the number of weeks worked (40 x 50 = 2000).

5. Divide your annual salary ($100,000) by the product in Step 4 (100,000 / 2000 = 50). This number shows how much your time is worth per hour. In this case, it's $50.

6. Apply the Drifting Coefficient depending on where you evaluate it on the map.

CASE STUDY TASK

TASK DESCRIPTION			
Bookkeeping			

COEFFICIENT	DRIFTING COST / HR	HOURS PER WEEK	COST PER YEAR
4	$200	2	$20K

Let's use bookkeeping as an example. In this case study, let's assume that you are, like most entrepreneurs, sub-par at bookkeeping (which is really good for most entrepreneurs). The sub-par zone has a 4X coefficient.

How many hours per week do you spend doing bookkeeping? Let's suppose it's two hours. Because we are using a 4X coefficient, you will multiply your hourly rate by four. That means this task isn't costing you $50 per hour, but $200 instead.

That's a total of $400 per week that your bookkeeping is really costing you in opportunity loss. This is what we call the Drifting Cost.

Now, let's say you work for 50 weeks every year. Because you have a Drifting Cost of $400 on bookkeeping each week, this adds up to $20,000 per year.

That's how much you're leaving on the table by staying in your sub-par zone and doing your own bookkeeping for two hours per week.

It's easy to rationalize Drifting Costs by saying, "I'm saving money by doing this myself." Here's the truth: you aren't. To continue with the bookkeeping example, consider this: Does hiring a bookkeeper from a small company cost $20,000 a year?

Certainly not. At most, it will cost a few hundred dollars per month, maybe even less if you use automation tools available with most bookkeeping software.

The take-home message is simple: You could be making more money while investing less energy in the process. As a new business owner, you may need to take on lots of tasks, and that's normal. But Drifting Costs can be huge, and you need to gradually remove these opportunity robbers and energy eaters from your plate. This is guaranteed to free you to focus on your area of power. For a lot of people, this exercise is a humbling experience. You're going to see exactly how many dollars you are missing out on every year.

The best approach is to outsource, automate, and delegate most of these tasks. The Effic method will teach you how to do this.

Calculating Drifting Costs is not an exact science, but the exercise you've just done will give a useful dollar value to work with. If you're an Effic Certified Partner, use this exercise with a client. They will quickly understand the real costs of trying to do tasks that they aren't good at.

To get the most from this process, I encourage you to track your hours for a week and record exactly how you spend your time. What tasks do you work on, and for how long? Take a comprehensive task inventory. For each task, ask yourself, "In what zone is this task, and what's the Drifting Cost of performing it on an annual basis?"

In the next module, we will be looking at the Impact Matrix. This is a fantastic tool that will help you identify the nature of a task and help you decide with precision what you should be focusing on. You'll discover which of your tasks give you the most bang for your buck, both financially and energetically.

Truth#4: Work-Life Balance Doesn't Work

Build a business around *your life, not a life around your business*. We've all heard this line, and many entrepreneurs try to take it on board. Maybe you're one of them. But what if I told you that this well-meaning piece of advice manages to be both right and wrong at the same time?

Being an entrepreneur is not like working as an employee. When it comes to managing your business and lifestyle, you need to take a completely different approach.

► Ditch The "Work-Life Balance"

Let's be honest—you don't work on your business during the day and then come home and live your life. There might be a clear line between home and work for employees, but not for entrepreneurs.

The notion of a "work-life balance" is damaging. It creates a negative perception around work, upholding the idea that "life" is good and "working" is bad. This is a nonsensical idea for creative entrepreneurs whose creativity is their gift to humanity.

The real enemy isn't work. The danger is a poor self-leadership style that results in a life dedicated solely to work.

The idea that "work" competes with "life" implies that they are always competing rather than coexisting. When we think of the word "balance," we think of a 50/50 split. The reality is that work and life are never 50/50. They inevitably overlap. Instead of focusing on the idea of work-life balance, I invite you to look at the issue from a holistic point of view.

► A Holistic View For An Integrated Lifestyle

Not all doctors take the same approach to health. Take the example of a medical doctor versus a naturopathic doctor. Both are health professionals. Both want to keep their patients healthy. However, they have different perspectives.

Medical doctors practice traditional medicine. They evaluate the human body, its disorders, and medical treatments in purely biophysical or biochemical terms. On the other hand, naturopathic doctors focus on holistic health. Holistic medicine does not focus on illness or specific parts of the body. This ancient style of medical practice considers the whole person and how he or she interacts with his or her environment. It emphasizes the connections between the mind, body, and spirit.

Entrepreneurship is not just a way of working. It's a way of being. You have to continually manage and measure multiple parameters like relationships, family time, wellness, education, projects, product development, meetings, and finances. Like a holistic doctor, you need to look beyond your day-to-day tasks and schedules, and take a well-rounded approach to life and work.

The key here is to achieve work-life harmony, not "balance." Think of work and life as yin and yang. This concept is based on an ancient dualist Chinese philosophy. The idea of yin and yang describes how seemingly opposite or contrary forces may actually be complementary, interconnected, and interdependent in the natural world and how they may give rise to each other through a dynamic relationship.

When it comes to work and life, there are no trade-offs, only a symbiotic order that serves both sides. Life will influence your business, and your business will shape your life. This harmony can only be sustained by responsible, thoughtful self-leadership.

Truth #5: Your Priorities Will Change

The ancient Greek philosopher Heraclitus once said, "Change is the only constant in life." We all have to adapt and evolve from year to year, and sometimes even from day to day. As you go through life and develop yourself as a person and entrepreneur, you need to accept that nothing will stay the same for long. Changes in your personal life or family situation, advancing age, and world events are all important opportunities to step back and assess your priorities.

► The Entrepreneurial Midlife Crisis

Although people can go through changes and personal upheaval at any age, it's common to go through a crisis in midlife. The term "midlife crisis" traditionally refers to a transition of self-confidence and identity that happens somewhere between a person's late 30s and late 40s. It's triggered by changes or events that remind them of their mortality and the passing of time.

If you have a midlife crisis, you might become obsessed with what you have and have not achieved. It can be painful to realize that you haven't met all of your goals, or that your life hasn't turned out quite as you planned it. A midlife crisis can trigger anxiety, depression, and regret. Some people decide to make dramatic changes to their lifestyles or try to recapture feelings of youth or adventure.

Entrepreneurial midlife crises are triggered by a combination of age, your level of entrepreneurial freedom, and where you are in your entrepreneurial journey. During the crisis, the entrepreneur starts thinking about how they will use their experience, knowledge, and leadership to leave behind a meaningful legacy. They realize, perhaps for the first time, that time is a finite resource. They become aware of their mortality and realize that the only power any of us have is to decide how we invest our energy and attention.

However, an entrepreneurial midlife crisis doesn't involve looking back to the past; it focuses on the future. It's a time of upheaval, but it also pushes the entrepreneur to become more impactful and reassess their priorities. It's an exciting period of evolution.

When you reach this stage in your journey, you'll rethink your definition of freedom. It's common to move away from a hustle-based mindset and focus on meaning instead. You'll realize that money can't buy health or time. It becomes less important, particularly if you've had financial freedom for a while. Most people chase money when they start a business, hoping to compensate for their insecurities or to build as much wealth as possible, but the novelty wears off.

Many entrepreneurs also start thinking about how they can simplify their work and lifestyle. Quality becomes more important than quantity. Instead of working "more," they begin to think about working "right." Many rethink their spending habits. They start allocating more money to meaningful, purposeful projects and pastimes. As they look to the future, living a sustainable lifestyle and running a sustainable business becomes more of a priority.

► Kids

In January 2014, my life changed forever when I became a dad. When our little girl entered our world, she upgraded it forever. Before you become a parent, you think you know what it will be like. The truth is, you have no idea what's coming. Your routines and habits will change. You will invest your energy and attention into the growth of your child rather than the growth of your business.

When you become a mom or dad, you suddenly gain a new identity: "mompreneur" or "dadpreneur." This doesn't mean your priorities are split between your business and your child. It just means that becoming a parent adds a new layer to your identity. You're faced with a new challenge: making sure your work and life are in harmony.

Having a baby changes every aspect of your life. Becoming a parent will force you to rethink your priorities. The most obvious change is the demands on your time. When you have a kid, they always have to come first. For example, evenings and weekends that might have been spent working will probably be taken up by family activities.

Your financial habits will also have to change. Because you'll now have to think about childcare costs, medical bills, college funds, and the other expenses that come with raising kids, you'll need to rethink your spending habits. You might have less to invest in your business.

Your child will take up most of your energy and attention, meaning you have less time for your work. To make sure you get everything done, you'll need to establish more structure in your life. Your daily and weekly routines will become more important than ever.

Having to take care of kids that depend on us to meet all their needs has changed me. When I became a parent, I realized that most things I do aren't really that important. It's forced me to realign my priorities and figure out my core values.

► Gaining Perspective

From personal experience, I can tell you that birth and death put everything into perspective, but other major, unforeseen events can also change your worldview.

For example, think about how you felt during the COVID-19 pandemic of 2020. You probably felt more inclined to tell your family that you love them and to check in on your friends to make sure they were OK. You might have started appreciating the little things in life, or taking time to notice the beauty in your surroundings. Perhaps you picked up a long-neglected hobby or even took up a brand new pastime. Rather than saying, "I'll do this when I'm not so busy," you started to seize the moment and start doing what you always wanted.

Challenging times like these give you a sense of perspective, highlight your values, and make you evaluate what is truly important to you. In general, values don't change. However, difficult times can become a transition period that has a profound impact on how we relate to life. It's possible that your core values might shift, but it's more likely that they will simply be re-ordered.

For example, sustainability has been (and continues to be) my most important core value. I don't see that changing anytime soon. Other values, however, have moved down and allowed for more authentic ones to surface. For me, the values of community and creativity have moved up the list in recent times.

The things you prize now will change, and may not be what you prioritize later. You can value something without it being part of your values. For example, you might value owning a sports car, but it's unlikely to have anything to do with your core values. When your core values shuffle around, the car will become irrelevant. The things you value will change based on your context. All too often, we hold on to possessions and material things that keep us out of alignment with our principles and core values.

When major events happen or a catastrophe strikes, we get some perspective. This shift influences how we approach life and business. As it has for so many other people, the global pandemic has definitely influenced my approach to work. It has helped me make decisions I would have delayed or maybe never have gotten around to making, and has been a turning point in my journey as an entrepreneur.

However, even when you have a pure and sincere desire to make significant changes and upgrade your life, your new determination always seems to slip away as you get back into your old routine. That's why it's crucial to establish a structure in your life that is sustainable and can accommodate these changes.

Part 2:
The Effic® Philosophy

The Secrets To Sustainable
Performance & Productivity

The Effic philosophy sums up everything we believe in, and it's what makes the methodology so unique and powerful.

Effic goes against today's entrepreneurial culture, which emphasizes extreme working practices, busyness, and constant "hustle." Most entrepreneurs think it's reasonable to work every day, to be obsessed with your business, and to neglect everything else in your life for the sake of putting in more hours and making more money. This is a recipe for misery and burnout, but most of us think it's the only way to succeed.

Our philosophy is entirely different. Unlike other leaders in the time management and productivity world, our approach will give you sustainable results. As you'll see, you don't have to sacrifice everything important for you to be a performant entrepreneur.

The Effic philosophy teaches you how to build sustainable bridges between your work, your life, and yourself. It's about mastering self-leadership, managing your workload, working more efficiently, and leveraging your strengths. The Effic philosophy empowers entrepreneurs to think about their lives and businesses from a different, healthier, and more holistic perspective. We aren't just entrepreneurs—we are human beings.

The Effic philosophy was inspired by my time in the sports performance world. Great athletes and successful entrepreneurs have a lot in common, and I applied what I learned as a physique athlete and coach when developing the Effic methodology. When we talk about the concept of the athlete entrepreneur, you'll quickly see the parallels between sports and business.

Let's start by looking at the first part of our philosophy: self-leadership.

You > Business
The Unselfish Art Of Self-Leadership

Leadership isn't only about how to lead and manage other people. There's another type of leadership you need to learn and develop as an entrepreneur: self-leadership.

Self-leadership involves getting to know yourself, building on your strengths, and taking the initiative when setting and working towards goals. It develops a sense of who you are as person, your skills and capacities, combined with the ability to shape your actions and decisions.

You can't separate your personal and public leadership. In other words, if you want to lead others, you must lead yourself first. Self-leaders tend to be emotionally sensitive towards themselves and others. They have excellent relationship skills, which is clearly a strong asset for any entrepreneur. If you lead a team, you need these skills when delegating tasks, giving feedback, and discussing ideas with others.

Because self-leadership involves understanding your strengths and weaknesses, it's directly linked to self-awareness. Everyone is a work in progress. When you lead yourself, you look at mistakes as learning opportunities. You can step back from a situation, take an objective look at what has happened, and decide what to do differently next time around. This is an essential step towards behavioral change, which ultimately builds healthy habits, routines, and drives success.

When you learn to lead yourself, you'll be able to cope better with stressful situations. You won't be caught in a state of reactivity. Instead, you'll be able to identify sources of stress early, choose how you want to handle them, remain in the moment, and calmly choose the best course of action. Because self-leadership means being honest with yourself, you'll also be free of the stress that comes from denying who you are.

Finally, self-leadership is crucial for alignment. When you know who you are and what you want, you'll know whether your current goals and behaviors are aligned with your goals. Self-leaders are willing to be accountable to themselves and others, which keeps them productive and motivated.

My journey as a physique athlete made me a better entrepreneur, helped grow my self-acceptance, and developed my self-leadership. From a young age, I felt "different." I didn't thrive in academic settings. My brain was bursting with ideas. Unfortunately, I couldn't express my creativity in school. I'm sure a lot of entrepreneurs will know what I'm talking about. As an adult, I still had lots of ideas, but I had a hard time harnessing my brainpower. I was disorganized and couldn't seem to complete any projects.

As entrepreneurs, we're different from other people, and that's not always easy to manage as we grow up. For me, school wasn't a pleasant experience. I had a hard time following the rules, and the classes didn't hold my attention. I didn't see the point in memorizing stuff for tests and then forgetting it all the next day.

Because traditional academic environments weren't a good fit for me, I was quickly labeled as someone who "wouldn't go very far in life." My parents always believed in me, but they weren't optimistic that I'd find a promising career path.

Back then, I didn't know that my reaction to the school system was typical for a future entrepreneur. I had entrepreneurial superpowers, but I didn't realize it. I think they are in every entrepreneur's DNA. We have a higher than average capacity for coming up with new ideas, seeing hidden opportunities, and finding creative solutions to problems.

We process things differently. Our brains are active volcanoes, always on the verge of erupting with new ideas. Unfortunately, this superpower is also one of our flaws. It means we are likely to spread ourselves too thinly because we try to do lots of things at once.

When I was younger, I was good at starting new projects, but I was terrible at finishing them. Fortunately, in my 20s, I got into fitness, which gave me the self-leadership I would later need as an entrepreneur. Without it, I wouldn't be where I am today. It gave me a sense of structure and discipline that many entrepreneurs lack when they start out in business. Fitness was the catalyst that made me fully aware of my superpowers and taught me to harness them.

I now know that self-leadership means treating yourself as a human being first and an entrepreneur second. It's about balancing your finite resources—time, attention, and energy—so you avoid burnout and maximize your performance.

Some people think that prioritizing yourself is selfish, but this simply isn't true. Self-leadership isn't self-indulgence. It's the first and most crucial step towards success in business and life. Without it, you'll drift off course and will struggle to lead anyone else. The most successful entrepreneurs and business people understand that growing your self-leadership is a good investment of your time. Your needs as a human being are just as important as the needs of your business. Personal and professional growth go hand in hand. Keep in mind that a company is only as good as its leader.

Developing self-leadership isn't a one-off exercise. It's a never-ending process that requires a complete change in mindset. To become great self-leaders, we need to continually develop three things: self-discipline, self-awareness, and self-respect. Let's take a closer look at each.

► Self-Discipline

According to the dictionary, self-discipline is "the ability to control one's feelings and overcome one's weaknesses; the ability to pursue what one thinks is right despite temptations to abandon it." Self-disciplined people push through discomfort when they need to get something done. They put their goals above short-term happiness or pleasure.

Self-discipline is not the same thing as motivation. Motivation is a desire to do something. When someone says they feel motivated to do their work, they actively want to do it.

They can't wait to get started, and they enjoy it. On the other hand, self-discipline is the ability to complete the work, even when things get tough. Motivation feels good, but you can't rely on it to keep you going. When it's gone, you have to fall back on self-discipline.

It's also important for behavioral change and establishing good habits. Having goals is a great start, but permanent behavior changes are essential if you want to harness your entrepreneurial superpowers.

Self-discipline leads to consistency, and consistency leads to permanent behavioral change. Self-leaders rely on habits, routines, and rituals in their personal and professional lives that work, and they are disciplined enough to follow them. This requires practice. The more times you repeat a behavior or routine, the easier it becomes.

Set yourself up to succeed by removing temptations in your environment. For example, if you tend to get distracted by social media when you're supposed to be working, download an app that blocks these sites for a specific period of time. Make it easy to make the right decisions. Your brain can only make a finite number of choices per day. If you follow a consistent schedule, it's easier to keep your focus.

Decide that you can tolerate discomfort. In the military, there's this concept called "embrace the suck," which is defined as to consciously accept or appreciate something extremely unpleasant but unavoidable. Some days, you won't feel like working on your business because you know you'll have to shovel manure. That's normal. A common mistake is to wait for motivation or inspiration to strike. Self-disciplined people don't do that. They push on, regardless of how they feel.

Self-disciplined people create mindful goals for themselves that align with their broader vision and move the needle in their business. In other words, they are proactive rather than reactive. We all have to deal with reactive tasks, but self-disciplined people get into the habit of dealing with them at a specific time. They don't get sucked into pointless meetings or email conversations. Instead, they get into the habit of following a schedule and a set of routines to deal with reactive tasks so that they don't eat up precious time that should be spent developing their business. The Effic methodology will show you how to do this.

► Self-Awareness

People who are self-aware acknowledge and understand their own perspectives, strengths, weaknesses, leadership potential, and emotional needs.

The reality is, lots of us lack self-awareness. Instead of acknowledging our strengths, taking pride in our unique skill set, and getting to know ourselves, we try to copy other people. We don't stay true to ourselves, and as a result, we don't reach our full potential. It's essential that you're willing to audit yourself honestly.

To be self-aware means accepting your shortcomings and accentuating your strengths. We are all different. Acknowledge what makes you stand out, and plan how you can leverage it. Look inside yourself and uncover your modus operandi. How do you operate? What are your behavioral patterns—both the ones that serve you and the ones you need to correct?

We are all complex human beings who crave purpose. What fulfills someone else might do absolutely nothing for you. Chasing the wrong goals and appropriating other people's ambitions will only leave you feeling empty. It's your responsibility as a self-leader to decide where you want to go, and what your core values are.

Once you've identified what it is you want, search deep inside yourself and ask yourself a simple question: "Why do I want this?" If you want to gain someone else's approval or admiration, you should think again. External feedback can be useful, but self-awareness and self-discovery is even more powerful.

Self-awareness is also a critical component of emotional intelligence (EQ), which is widely recognized as a key to business success in the 21st century. First introduced to the public in the 1990s by writer and psychologist Daniel Goleman, EQ is defined as the ability to understand and handle your own emotions and those of other people. People high in EQ are socially skilled, capable of handling stressful situations, and can easily build positive relationships with other people. Unsurprisingly, they tend to make good self-leaders who excel at managing others.

► Self-Respect

To have self-respect is to feel proud about who you are, and to have confidence in yourself. Self-respect comes when you feel you are behaving with honor and dignity. It's about living in line with your values, beliefs, and talents. Until you respect yourself, you can't harness the power of self-discipline and self-awareness.

Self-respect is also about honoring the process as you progress along your personal and entrepreneurial journey. Your visions and ambitions need to be in alignment with your core values and truth. You need the courage to understand who you are, honor what you want, and work towards it.

Respect your entrepreneurial brain. Personally, I had a hard time respecting myself for a long time because I wasn't academically accomplished. I assumed that because I hadn't done very well at school, I wouldn't succeed in life. These days, I don't treat my crazy and weird brain like a liability. It's an asset I need to care for. Honor your limitations and strengths.

Finally, respect your energy. Even the most hardworking and enthusiastic entrepreneurs can't work 24/7. You need to accept that your mind and body need time to rest and recover. Pushing yourself all the time is a recipe for burnout. Lots of entrepreneurs forget that they are human, and they end up overwhelmed and miserable. Don't make that mistake. As you apply the Effic methodology, you'll learn how to put your needs and wellbeing at the center of everything you do.

In short, self-leadership is not about being the best. It's the ongoing process of creating the conditions to be at your best so you can make your business and everyone else better. This is what my time as a physique athlete taught me. I've learned to create a structure that allows me to develop and maintain high levels of self-discipline, self-awareness, and self-respect. In the next chapter, I will show you the techniques I learned and borrowed from the world of sports performance that helped me become an effective self-leader.

The Athlete Entrepreneur
3 Timeless Sports Performance Techniques
Applied To Entrepreneurship

My journey as a physique athlete made me a better entrepreneur. Through physical transformation, I learned the tools I needed for self-leadership. This would prove essential to my success. When young entrepreneurs ask me how to get started, my answer is always the same: "Transform your body."

Elite entrepreneurs and athletes are very similar. Both develop extraordinary self-leadership. Both have a set of skills and talents that they never take for granted. They take self-development seriously and never stop learning. Both know that their work ethic and passion give them an edge over their rivals, and they strive to beat both their competitors and who they were yesterday.

Athletes and entrepreneurs must both learn the art of systems thinking. Just as an athlete must learn how to manage their strengths and weaknesses and their role within a team, an entrepreneur must learn how to set up systems within their business to keep everything running smoothly. As your business grows, you'll need to continually adjust your systems, just as an athlete adjusts their training schedule to prepare them for an event or season.

As an entrepreneur, you should expect to fail and to fail often. Athletes never win every game or hit the target every time, and it's the same in business. Avoiding failure isn't an option; it's about how you deal with setbacks, even under pressure, that makes all the difference. It's important to learn from failure, but not to dwell on your mistakes. The best athletes always focus on their next game or their next shot. As an entrepreneur, you also need to always be on the lookout for opportunities. Just because you find something difficult right now doesn't mean you can't improve.

No matter what their sport, a great athlete doesn't work alone, and neither does a great entrepreneur. An athlete may have a coach, a nutritionist, a physiotherapist, and the support of their teammate. Entrepreneurs often look to mentors, guides, and people with more experience in their industry. Athletes rely on feedback to improve. They are used to criticism, and the best performers don't take it personally. Successful entrepreneurs have a similar attitude. They listen to their customers, their business partners, and their mentors, knowing that feedback is a springboard to success.

In both sport and business, preparation and organization are vital. Athletes and entrepreneurs can't afford to rely on vague plans and hope. They need sustainable and well-constructed schedules that are broken down into days, weeks, months, quarters, seasons, or years. As the famous adage goes, "If you fail to prepare, you are preparing to fail." It takes a lot of mental grit to stick with a challenging schedule, and this mental resilience is something they cultivate.

As an entrepreneur, you need to be in it for the long haul. Just as it takes an athlete years of training to reach the highest level, an entrepreneur shouldn't expect overnight success.

The world of sports performance was a major source of inspiration for us when creating the Effic methodology. We've taken three timeless performance techniques and applied them to entrepreneurship. Taken together, they will give you a strong foundation for developing self-leadership skills and enjoying sustainable success.

► Technique #1: Load Management

In June 2019, the Toronto Raptors became the first team outside the United States to become NBA Champions. It had been 26 years since Canada won a major sports championship when my beloved Montreal Canadiens won the Stanley Cup in 1993. Thousands of Toronto fans danced in the streets after their team won the best of seven series by four games to two against the Golden States Warriors, who had won 3 championships over the past four seasons.

Raptors forward Kawhi Leonard played a vital role in his team's win, but his acquisition in the summer of 2018 was a bold move. Leonard suffered an injury during the 2017/2018 season, playing in just nine matches.

Team president Masai Ujiri faced significant backlash after bringing him on board. Fans were uneasy with the decision to invest in a player with his injury record, especially after sending crowd favorite DeMar DeRozan to San Antonio in exchange for Leonard.

Leonard also attracted attention for spending a lot of time on the bench. He sat out 22 of 81 games in the 2018-2019 season.

However, his absences were all part of a more comprehensive strategy: load management, a well-known concept in the world of sports science but unknown to the general public. The fact that he missed games while having no "apparent" injuries caused controversy around the world of basketball, causing Leonard to be labeled as someone with a questionable work ethic who didn't have enough love for the game. It's comparable to what we see in business culture. If you don't appear to be always working, you're labeled as lazy and not driven enough.

What Exactly Is Load Management?

Load management is an approach to preventing injury while maximizing performance. "Load" refers to anything that places a demand on an athlete. A load can be external or internal. An external load is anything applied to the athlete, like a training session. External load can be measured without reference to the individual's characteristics. An internal load is defined as a physiological or psychological response to an external stimulus.

A high training load, combined with frequent competitive events, can impair both short and long-term performance. Load management helps an athlete build their strength and workload tolerance gradually.

The Raptors' sports science director and assistant coach, Alex McKechnie, is credited for Leonard's success. From the beginning of Leonard's time with the team, he carefully monitored the player's workload, fitness, and general health. He slowly increased the demands on Leonard, which kept his injury risk low.

McKechnie wasn't afraid to bench the player for the good of his health. During the season, Leonard never played both halves of a back-to-back. His teammates commented that sometimes they didn't know whether he was playing until the final few minutes before a game.

The Stats Speak For Themselves

Leonard's load management paid off. He is currently one of the best players on the planet, with an enviable and ever-growing list of records to his name. Following the Raptors' victory, he earned his second Finals MVP Award.

Over the playoffs, he was an absolute beast: He averaged 30.9 points, 4 assists, 1.7 steals, and 9.2 rebounds per game. His total score is only 27 points short of the all-time record held by none other than Michael Jordan. Leonard has also become one of just seven players who have averaged 30 points for at least 20 games while maintaining a minimum 50% field goal percentage.

In short, he's a fantastic example of load management in action. Proper load management ensures you can unlock top performance when you need it most. When you have a proper structure, you shine. It's about unleashing top performance at the right time, as Kawhi did during the playoffs.

How Do You Apply Load Management To Entrepreneurship?

It's simple: Load management is critical for sustainable performance. It's the most important concept you need to understand. Everything you'll learn in this book aligns with this principle.

For too long, we've praised the people who work the hardest. This is no longer the case. Our generation is starting to realize that a more personalized approach to work yields better results. Most people focus on short-term results. Don't do that. Instead, put together a bigger, better, long-term game plan.

This strategy will demand patience. If you're serious about succeeding as an entrepreneur, you'll need to learn to grow over time instead of placing yourself under constant pressure. Don't ask too much of yourself too soon.

1. Get Control Over Your Workload

When you exercise, pushing yourself as hard and often as possible is never a smart strategy. It's a common beginner's mistake in both sports and business. You need time to adjust to new workloads. If you are an entrepreneur, overloading yourself with too many tasks is exactly like overtraining.

Overtraining happens when a person's body has exceeded its ability to recover from a demanding exercise. Their performance declines and plateaus because they can't consistently perform at a certain level or handle a training load that exceeds their recovery capacity.

Yes, people can cope with high loads, but only if two conditions are met. First, they must be given the right training. Second, they must be allowed to adapt. Imagine what would happen if I were to ask someone who had never worked out before to bench press 220 lbs during their first-ever training session. Do you think I could expect them to walk away uninjured? No. It often takes months to grow the kind of muscle mass needed for that kind of performance. It also requires patience and a willingness to take rest days.

Most people overestimate how much they can carry. Don't be an ego lifter. You need to carry a workload that matches your capacity and give yourself time to breathe between assignments.

Like promises of overnight muscle growth, "overnight productivity" is a scam. Trying to do too much too quickly will always blow up in your face. However, when you devote yourself to handling things strategically and increasing your work in measured doses, you grow your ability to handle stress and deliver results. You can do this safely, so you don't have to risk hurting yourself.

You should be able to tell when you have more work on your plate than you can handle. I don't want to discourage you or focus too much on your limits. I simply want to emphasize that the best kind of growth is achieved over time through an intelligent structure and a thoughtful approach to workload management. The next strategy in this book, Periodization, explores this idea in greater depth.

2. Monitor Your Responses

The first step to improving anything, including your work, is to track it. It's like getting fit. As you train, you need to monitor the right parameters so you can get better results. For example, you might monitor how much weight you lift, the number of repetitions you can do, your bodyfat percentage, the nutritional breakdown of your meals, and so on.

As entrepreneurs, we also need to track several key parameters. First, you need to track your energetic response to a type of task. In other words, does a task energize or drain you? In this context, "energetic" doesn't just mean your physical response. You need to consider mental and emotional responses too. Next, you need to understand how you respond to various types of schedules. We need to monitor what type of routine is the best fit for your personality and strengths. Finally, you'll also need to track what kind of work environment keeps you most focused.

Lots of people find it tricky to monitor their responses, especially when it comes to mental and emotional responses. It's vital that you make it a long-term habit. Over time, you'll identify patterns and develop a newfound self-awareness. I can't emphasize this point enough: Self-awareness is probably the most crucial factor to success.

3. Make contextual adjustments

No people have the same work capacity. What's more, capacity can vary; it's subject to the influence of internal and external factors. As human beings, we have to deal with life's ups and downs. Our total load goes beyond work. We all have to deal with personal challenges from time to time. We'll discuss this further in the Life & Business Harmony section.

For now, consider this quote by coach Alex McKechnie: "You can't control trauma. Trauma will happen, but you can mitigate some of the damages." Everyone, even your star performers, experience unplanned setbacks and injuries. You won't always be in peak condition, and you must make the same allowance for others.

Sometimes, internal and external factors mean you'll have to make decisions that will change your short-term plans. You'll need to be flexible, but it pays off. In the long run, both you and your business will win.

In summary, effective workload management forms the foundation of productivity and performance. It must underpin everything you do. Both your day-to-day decisions and long-term strategy depend on your ability to master this skill. Take it seriously

► Technique #2: Periodization

Periodization is the process of dividing an annual training plan into smaller blocks. Each block is geared toward a particular goal. To meet the goal, you must put your body under different types of stress. This allows you to mix harder and easier training periods in a way that facilitates recovery and maximizes performance.

Periodized training is based on the concept of overload and adaptation. By stressing the body over time, allowing it to recover, and then stressing it again, an athlete will gradually build up their fitness. When properly orchestrated, periodization ensures that athletes are at their peak when it matters most.

Typically, periodization is broken down into 3 phases:

1. The Macrocycle - In athletics, a macrocycle is a whole season. This is the longest of all the periodization phases, typically spanning a year. A macrocycle covers all core aspects of the typical athlete's training regimen, such as intensity, speed, endurance, competition, and recovery. To map out a macrocycle is to get a bird's-eye view that enables long-range planning.

2. The Mesocycle - A mesocycle is a training block within a season that is designed to accomplish a particular goal. This typically spans several weeks.

3. The Microcycle - A microcycle refers to the smallest unit within a mesocycle. In most cases, it's a week of training. This week is broken down further into training blocks that include specific movements and actions.

A periodized structure will always get results

Periodization is the key to strategic alignment. In other words, it helps you work out precisely what you must do to reach the goals that support your vision. When you use a periodized work structure, you won't have to keep stopping to wonder what you are supposed to be doing next. Instead of rethinking and reinventing your plans on a weekly or even daily basis, you can focus on the road ahead. If you use periodization, you'll be proactive instead of frazzled and overwhelmed. It eliminates all guesswork and saves you a considerable amount of time and mental energy.

It gives you a clear proactive plan

A periodized structure eliminates guesswork and gives you clear steps to follow. It will allow you to keep track of your behaviors, responses, and outcomes. This grows your self-awareness, which is essential to your success. It's an excellent opportunity to learn about yourself, as well as your specific needs and skills. Remember the golden rule: what gets measured, gets improved.

Careful tracking will also help you assess your workload based on capacity and demand, just like an athlete varies their training schedule as they move between in-season versus off-season periods.

It helps you adapt and make you more performant over time.

Periodization helps you adapt to a workload, which in turn will make you more efficient. Adaptation occurs when your body gets accustomed to a particular exercise program or training load through repeated exposure. As your body adapts to the stress of the new exercise or training program, the program becomes easier to perform.

People who are new to exercise are often sore after starting a new routine. However, after doing the same exercise for weeks and months at the same intensity, they experience little, if any, muscle soreness. This is because their bodies have adapted.

Adaptation means we require less energy to perform the same exercise that we previously found demanding.

Your progress will plateau if you keep doing the same things over and over again for too long. To maximize your results, you need to continually vary the exercise and training routine as you become more efficient. That's why we build mesocycles.

How To Apply Periodization To Entrepreneurship

1. **Have a long-term vision and decide on your annual objectives**

Create your first macrocycle by clarifying a long-term vision that aligns with your annual objectives. Only by doing this will you stay on track and get the right results. You'll need to specify precisely what you want to accomplish and know in advance how you'll quantify the results. We'll look at how you can do this when we get to the first step of the Effic Method.

2. **Work in 90-day cycles**

You need to set the outcomes you want to achieve in 90 days' time and then, using reverse engineering, draw up realistic sub-goals and timelines to get you there. For each quarter, you'll need to prioritize your projects, so they align with your overall vision.

As a fitness coach, I've met many people who want to build muscle or lose fat fast but aren't willing to commit to a plan. As a business consultant, it's a similar story. I've met many leaders who are too obsessed with getting quick results, jumping from one tactic to another, and never making real progress.

Whether you're a solopreneur or running a more prominent company, pushing forward without a solid structure in place is asking for disaster. 90-day cycles are also common in the business world as it typically works in financial quarters. A 90-day period gives you enough time to make significant headway and adapt to a workload. If you commit to reviewing your progress and setting new goals every 90 days, you will stay focused on what matters most. We'll look at this topic in greater depth in Step 2 of the Effic Method.

3. **Design an appropriate weekly schedule and daily action plan.**

My friend and Canadian performance coach Scott Abel has a saying: "A program is not a collection of exercises." So many entrepreneurs fill up their "to-do" lists with tasks but never get the results they want because they don't structure their work. They have long-term and medium-term goals but ultimately fail to follow a plan.

This haphazard approach is like going to the gym, doing random exercises, and hoping that you'll somehow achieve your fitness goals. Without a structured program, you won't see results. You must follow a properly adapted workout program.

Planning is vital, but it's only useful if you know how to do it effectively. Structuring your work, sticking to the plan, and learning how to perform your tasks properly will ensure your success each quarter. We'll cover this in more detail when we get to Step 3 of the Effic Method.

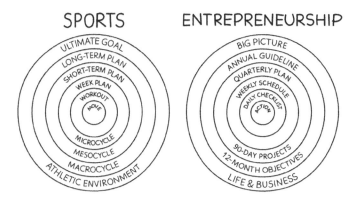

By thinking about your work in terms of cycles, as shown above, you'll be able to use effective load management and simultaneously increase your performance over time. You'll benefit from being able to track your progress in measurable terms, with the extra advantage of building strong adaptability. You'll get more work done than ever before but, because you've become more efficient, you'll actually expend less effort.

As an entrepreneur, I cannot overemphasize the benefits of applying periodization to your personal schedule and annual business objectives. By employing this principle correctly, you'll be able to break down complex projects into manageable bits. You'll ensure that a job gets done in good time without losing sight of other engagements. The power of periodization is that it lets you optimize both your short-term and long-term goals for maximum success.

► Technique #3: Rest & Recovery

If you play a sport or work out regularly, you're probably already aware that rest and recovery periods are key to staying healthy and improving your performance.

Most people think that rest and recovery is passive. They assume that all you have to do is take a break from your workouts or playing sports. But it's not quite that simple. To get the most from rest and recovery, you have to integrate this principle at multiple levels, taking into account both your short-term and long-term goals.

What is Rest & Recovery?

In sport, rest and recovery is a process that happens between periods of exertion. During this period, you give your body the chance to physically, mentally, and emotionally recover in preparation for your next session.

For optimum recovery, you need to actively manage your rest and recovery. The right approach will not only allow your muscles and connective tissue to repair, but it will also improve your fitness. If you haven't fully recovered from an exercise session, your next one will be a waste. Your performance will not improve if you don't understand and respect this principle.

Rest & Recovery Is The Key To Sustainable Growth Without Burning Out

People often think that training harder is the only way to improve your performance. There is a grain of truth here. Training, just like working on your business, requires effort.

However, you mustn't overlook rest and recovery. It's an essential part of the mix. Your body is only capable of so much in any one session. Training too much, or overtraining, will slow down your progress and can even cause burnout. The best athletes understand this. Unfortunately, amateurs often overlook rest and recovery.

Along with a well-structured exercise regimen, rest and recovery is essential for sustainable performance. It must be an integrated part of your plan. When duly incorporated, it will significantly improve your game.

How To Apply Rest & Recovery To Entrepreneurship

1. **Create habits, routines, and rituals**

You need to develop built-in lifestyle and business habits, routines, and rituals that promote a consistently high level of performance. As an entrepreneur, rest and recovery should be fully integrated into your everyday life. You need to manage and recharge your energy on all fronts: physical, mental, and emotional. Your body, your mind, and your spirit all need proper care.

2. **Proactively sync rest and recovery with your periodization cycles**

Rest and recovery should be integrated into your periodization cycles. Just as it gives your muscles the chance to heal when you're building fitness, it's mandatory if you want to unlock the power of adaptation.

Incorporate ongoing evaluation and review of your work progress into your periods of rest and recovery. A period of downtime presents a perfect opportunity to evaluate what you have achieved, whether it be over the past day, week, quarter, or even the past year.

It's also a good time to reflect on your personal growth and progress. As we discussed earlier, when we talked about the Principle of Adaptation, when we undergo the stress of physical exercise, our body adapts and becomes more efficient.

This principle applies when you learn any new skill. It's challenging at first, but over time it becomes second nature. You need to understand that during your adaptation process, you might need some extra rest and recovery. There are limits to how much stress someone can tolerate before they break down. Only by listening to yourself will you understand your personal limits.

3. Make it an asset you can't trade

When you have a proper work structure in place, you will inevitably perform to a higher standard. When your performance improves, you'll start seeing success. With success comes opportunities. That's right: When you make excellent progress, your reward is often the chance to take on more work.

When they reach this stage, almost all entrepreneurs start sacrificing their rest and recovery. Instead of balancing work with rest, they keep pushing themselves as they pursue new opportunities. This is often driven by FOMO (Fear Of Missing Out).

You'll likely feel guilty if you don't accept the new work that comes your way. But don't fall into this trap, even if your natural entrepreneurial instincts and our entrepreneurial culture tell you to go for it. You must regard rest and recovery as an untradable asset. It requires the same level of commitment as every other element of your plan. Overlooking it will always have negative long-term consequences.

For any entrepreneur who wants to perform at a sustainable level, there is no substitute for rest and recovery. This is one of the most crucial pieces of advice you should take from this book.

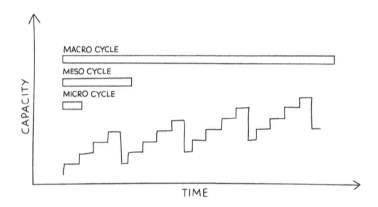

Pay close attention to many ways we incorporate it throughout the Effic Methodology, especially in the 4th Step of the Effic Method: Protection.

Efficiency First Productivity
The Forgotten Practice Of Working Right

Work is typically measured using the classic productivity formula. This formula calculates the rate of output per unit of input. In other words, it measures how production inputs, such as labor and capital, yield a particular level of output.

The way you think about and use this productivity formula will dictate how you work.

To achieve sustainable performance, you need to understand what real productivity looks like so you can work in the RIGHT way.

► Activity ≠ Productivity

We live in a world that glorifies the idea of "more" when it comes to working. Our modern entrepreneurial culture encourages extreme behaviors, such as putting in an excessive number of hours into your business and working yourself to the point of burnout. It completely disregards human needs and differences in an individual's capacity. If you adopt this attitude, you'll confuse activity with productivity. You'll assume that it's possible to gauge your productivity by simply measuring how much work you do.

As entrepreneurs, it's easy for us to fall into this trap without even realizing it. It usually happens on an unconscious level. We might not be able to explain why, but we know that if we don't produce as much work as we can, we'll be judged negatively by others in our community. They'll tell us, in subtle or not so subtle ways, that we don't belong in their elite group of "business leaders." The message is clear: If you're not a hustler, then you're not worthy as an entrepreneur.

But there's a better way to think about work and productivity. Consider how a production machine works. Imagine you set up a machine to create as much output as physically possible. In this scenario, the input refers to the maximum load of raw materials you could feed into the machine. If you decided to measure productivity in terms of quantity, you would keep inputting more and more raw materials into the engine in the hope of maximizing its output. If you took this approach, you would be working under the assumption that the best possible outcome is to keep producing as much output as possible in the shortest amount of time, even though this would mean sacrificing quality.

Here's the sad truth about running a machine at full speed at all times: it will break. A machine forced to continually grind raw materials will wear out. The more you max out your machine, the faster it depreciates from wear and tear. Eventually, it will fall apart.

Now think about how this principle applies to yourself as a human. Does it feel like you're always pushing hard without getting good results? Does your output fall short of your hopes and expectations?

Here's a crucial lesson to take on board: Shifting your mindset around productivity is essential if you want to perform sustainably. To do this, you have to carefully look at both ends of the equation, taking into account both input and output.

► Output Efficacy

First, you need to ask yourself the RIGHT questions:

> *What do you want to accomplish?*
> *What do you want out of your business?*
> *What does it look like in the end?*

Your desired outcome will dictate what you'll need to do. It doesn't work the other way around. Before you even assemble your resources, you need to be clear on what you want to build. Only when you have a clear, specific answer can you look at what's required to create it.

► Input Efficiency

Once you've established your desired outcome, you'll have to look at what it will take to obtain it. You'll need to focus on building efficiency. To be efficient is to avoid wasting resources when working to achieve a desired result. It is the ability to do things well, successfully, and without waste.

As entrepreneurs, on a human level, we have to look closely at how we manage these three precious and finite resources: time, energy, and attention. Time is an external resource, which means it's not something we own. Energy and Attention are internal resources, meaning that we have a level of control over these resources. Efficiency entails using the appropriate and responsible amount of these resources to reach your goals.

Efficiency is not about inputting as few finite resources as possible. Instead, it is about ensuring that you put in the RIGHT amount of time, energy, and attention based on your desired outcome and context.

> **The key is to understand how much <u>energy</u> you'll need, based on where you direct your <u>attention</u>, and organize your efforts according to the <u>time</u> you have available.**

Making these calculations, understanding this principle, and thinking carefully about improving your efficiency is part of the self-awareness process. As your self-awareness grows and you understand how you operate as an entrepreneur, the principle of adaptation kicks in through your periodized schedules, ensuring that your capacity grows at a consistent level. This is the best way to enjoy a sustainable performance.

Over time, this effect compounds. As you become more efficient, it will be easier to produce your desired outcome. You won't have to use so much energy. The beautiful by-product of this approach is a new ability to tap into these energy reserves to achieve your desired output in less time. Speed in business can be an extremely great asset. It's like having a nitro button. When everyone is racing and maxed out, only you have access to this resource. It puts you at an unfair advantage.

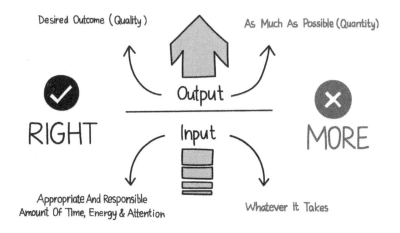

In summary, productivity is not about maxing out your efforts at every opportunity. Being productive is actually about knowing where you're headed and using the appropriate and responsible amount of finite resources to get there.

Your mindset needs to shift from *As Much As Possible* to *As RIGHT As Possible.* RIGHT management of your finite resources over time will let you achieve the RIGHT results, which is how you'll achieve truly sustainable productivity.

The Three Ss Of Leverage

Using Strengths, Structure and
Systems To Create Space

We all get 24 hours per day. Time is a finite, external resource that's beyond our control. We can't get more of it, we can't store it, and we can't reuse it.

Fortunately, we can control our internal resources. Everyone can choose how and where to direct their energy and attention. To make the most of your time, you must learn how to leverage it.

► The Three Ss Of Leverage

Leverage is a fantastic force. With just a little pressure, we can multiply our abilities and impact. The art of leverage is a ticket to freedom. It lifts the burden of recurring tasks that can weigh you down.

To show you exactly how to apply it, we use the three Ss: Strengths, Structure, and Systems.

Let's take a look.

Identify & Prioritize <u>Strengths</u>

As you'll see later in this book with the Impact Matrix, choosing the right high-impact tasks will create fantastic results for your business and will help you avoid drifting. To do this, you first need to identify and prioritize your strengths and those of others. When it comes to running your business, you will know better than anyone how everything fits together. However, you won't necessarily be the best person for a particular task. You need to understand your unique abilities and focus on them, but it's also vital that you leverage the individual competencies of the people around you.

You might not know your real strengths. It takes introspection, self-awareness, and time to understand where your talents lie. Remember, you must adhere to the "lead yourself first" philosophy. Self-leadership is the foundation of success.

So, what makes you truly great? Think about the core skills and abilities that inspired you to create your business. You became an entrepreneur for a reason. Doing what you are uniquely qualified to do will add so much value to your business.

Create A <u>Structure</u> That Will Allow These Strengths To Shine

Without structure, you won't get far in business or in life. Structure is like glue. It holds everything together. When you find a structure that works well for you, your days will be productive and aligned with your goals. You'll know that, however long the journey, you're on the right track.

The typical entrepreneurs start their own businesses because they want to be free of the typical 9-5. They don't want a boss breathing down their neck. They don't want to live by anyone else's schedule. Many entrepreneurs rebel against even the idea of structure, thinking that it will rob them of their personal and professional freedom.

But this is a dangerous way to think. Without a solid structure in place, your business cannot perform or grow sustainably. As paradoxical as it sounds, structure is the path to freedom.

Structure creates space, and space creates freedom. Structure lets you take back control over your time. It allows you to innovate and enjoy creative autonomy. With time, creative freedom equates to financial freedom. When you give yourself the space to leverage your strengths, your business will grow rapidly. You'll have the chance to use your unique superpowers, enjoy your freedom, and excel as an entrepreneur.

Develop <u>Systems</u> To Multiply The Effectiveness Of Your Structure

A system is a set of principles or procedures that determine how something is done. It's an organized scheme or method that brings order to chaos. When you learn to develop robust systems, you'll enhance the structure that gives you space.

Systems without structure is like exercising without a program. It works, but there is no way to track and improve. That's why the methods you'll learn here all have a coherent place and reason.

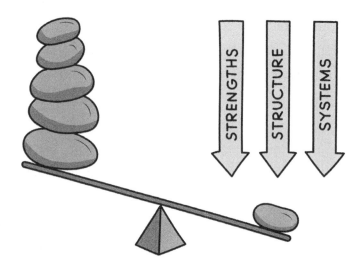

To sum it up, following our productivity and performance philosophy, being Effic is the state of SUSTAINABLY leveraging STRENGTHS using SYSTEMS within a STRUCTURE that gives you SPACE.

Now that you know our view on entrepreneurial life and business, it's time to dive into the methodology that will show you how to apply it to yourself.

Part 3:
The Effic® Method

The 4 Steps To Consistently
Achieve More By Noon
Than Other Entrepreneurs
In A Full Day

First, I want to answer a question that you have probably been asking yourself since you started reading this book: Where does the word "Effic" come from?

Effic is short for two words that sum up our approach. Here are these words and their definition from the dictionary:

- **Efficiency:** *To accomplish something with the least waste of time, effort, and resources.*

- **Efficacy:** *The ability to produce a desired or intended result or outcome.*

The Effic methodology is based on a simple goal: To create and protect a structure that will allow you to responsibly manage your time, energy, and attention in order to become a sustainably productive and performant self-leader while offering you the space needed to live a fulfilled entrepreneurial life. The Effic methodology consists of 4 steps:

1. Projection: In this stage, you will find your point of alignment for your business and your life. It involves projecting yourself into the future, understanding what you truly want, and committing it to paper in order to have a clear direction.

2. Prioritization: You'll learn how to prioritize the tasks that will make the most significant impact in your business, and understand what's truly important to focus on.

3. Planning: This is the most practical phase. You'll create an action plan for what you need to do on a daily, weekly, monthly, and quarterly basis to meet your goals.

4. Protection: In this phase, you'll learn how to protect your structure so it stays on track, looks after your health, works sustainably, and remains in alignment with your broader vision.

Entrepreneurship is a journey. Each journey starts with a vision of a destination. In this vision, we want something that currently lies beyond our reach. Our vision will influence every step we'll take and every decision we'll make along the way. Unless you're clear about where you're heading, you're just wandering purposelessly on the highway of entrepreneurship.

This is the starting point of a new fulfilling journey, and it's where we're starting our Effic adventure.

Step One

Projection

effic☑

In order to establish a clear direction, we're going to focus on two key components when it comes to long-term goals.

In the Projection phase, you'll need to do two things:

1. Create your Big Picture

2. Create your Annual Guideline

At Effic, we don't do traditional 10-year or 5-year plans. It's essential to have this kind of strategy when it comes to your finances because you want to understand the key growth metrics in your business, but the Big Picture and Annual Guideline offer a more holistic, flexible approach. They keep you in alignment even when your circumstances change.

The first component is called the Big Picture. It will help you decide what you truly want for yourself and your business. It will help you identify where you want to make an impact, and even what it is you live for. This will become your main point of alignment for your business and your life. It's the ultimate expression of self-awareness.

We all have this sense of direction within us, but we don't always know how to explain or verbalize it. Sometimes we just get sucked into the entrepreneurial universe and try to do too much. We start operating on wants and goals that aren't necessarily our own. It's important to understand what you truly want.

From there, we'll create an Annual Guideline. This means setting a series of goals for the coming year that are aligned with the Big Picture. It's simple but very powerful. When you review it over time, you'll realize that you are no longer drifting. We've talked about how much it costs you financially and energetically to drift in your business, so you know how important it is to avoid it.

Alignment 101

A Compass For Your Life & Business

Alignment is the act of linking your personal and professional goals. This requires a good understanding of what you want to achieve and why. To help you navigate your journey, we'll need to build a system that can keep you moving in the right direction at all times. Think of it as a compass for your life and business, something that always points at your magnetic north. It ensures you always know where you're going, and that you always have the right directions.

The fastest way to get somewhere is to go in a straight line. However, life and business don't work like that. You will have to face some roadblocks, pivot, change course, and venture down side roads you never thought you'd ever take. This is part of the journey. Everyone goes through it. Successful people are those who can enjoy the drive, even though it's not going exactly as planned, without getting lost along the way.

The goal is to create a big vision and a road map for you. We always use the analogy of a drive, which you'll already know if you're familiar with some of our more advanced concepts at Effic, such as the self-driving business.

Before we hit the road, here are some crucial points to understand:

► Your Business Is Your Vehicle

When you shop for a car, how do you pick the right model?

For some of us, look, speed, and acceleration are most important. For others, it is:

- Sustainability - what kind of impact does the car have on the environment?
- Efficiency - how far can you travel on a tank of gas?
- Comfort - is it nice to drive?

Your destination and context will ultimately determine which type of car is most appropriate for you. Have you ever tried making a long trip with kids in a sports car? It's not a great idea. Although a minivan isn't as fast, sexy, or flashy, it's a much better option for a family vacation. You need to decide the performance parameters based on what you want to get out of your car and why you're buying it.

You should take the same approach with your business. Most entrepreneurs use the wrong metrics to measure their performance. Just as a minivan doesn't have to cover a quarter-mile in 9.2 seconds or reach speeds of over 200 mph, don't apply irrelevant numbers when assessing how your business is doing. For example, some entrepreneurs might decide to measure their success in terms of how much money they are making, but that doesn't mean it's the most important metric for you.

Keep in mind that a car is only as good as its driver. If you're reckless in your life, you'll probably be a reckless driver. It's the same for your business. Your actions will dictate how well your business will run. The process of becoming a good self leader is the same as becoming a good driver. It takes practice, focus, and discipline.

► The Mountain Is Your Destination

What's the first thing you always do before going on a trip? You set a destination. As obvious as that sounds, many people still drive around without knowing where they're going. They don't keep their sights on a mountain, so they don't have a clear point of alignment.

Anyone who desires success must know precisely what they want. Your wants let you know how big your dream should be.

The truth is that other people will tell you to aim for other mountains that they think look more appealing. But it's up to you to choose your destination. Be aware that only you can decide how you'd like to experience your journey. When you let other people influence your destination, you set yourself up for a long and bumpy ride.

In the entrepreneurial world, there's a lot of bragging. People show off their successes and victories. They don't necessarily show the less glorious parts of entrepreneurship. We tend to look at these people, idealize them, or even idolize them. We think, "This is how I should operate," and we make their ambitions our own. I called this ambition appropriation. It's easy to assume that if they're doing something, we should be doing it too.

Don't do that. Own your own ambitions. We have one life to live, and our business is a reflection of who we are as individuals. They are an extension of ourselves.

If you look in the dictionary, you'll see that *success* is defined as "accomplishing an aim or purpose." *Fulfillment* is defined as "being satisfied or happy because of fully developing one's abilities or character." It's essential to understand the difference.

The bottom line is that when you align your performance with your purpose while finding happiness, you win. Genuinely successful people believe in what they are doing. They are comfortable in the car they're driving and are confident in their driving skills. Don't be embarrassed by what makes you unique.

► The Road Is Your Journey To Success

There is a quote from Tony Robbins that goes, "Success without fulfillment is the ultimate failure."

I couldn't agree more.

Personal fulfillment is the achievement of life goals that are important to an individual, in contrast to the goals of their society or family. Personal fulfillment is an ongoing journey, not a final destination.

This is why, when you set goals, you need to consider two things:

1. You need to ensure they are in line with your mountain (i.e., your destination).
2. You need to find the emotional angle for your goal to excite you on a personal level.

There is always an emotional element to our goals. It is not about the goal itself; it's about how it makes you feel.

We've all heard of entrepreneurs who built great businesses but then had their core values completely shift after a life-altering event. They no longer get any emotional thrill from building wealth, and the original motivation behind their goals evaporates.

It happened to me.

I remember vividly the words of my business partner.

"Dave, what do you want?" he asked.

"I just want to be happy, Matt," I replied. Matt had been my business partner for many years. Together, we operated a natural supplements business that was very financially successful.

However, for quite some time, I had felt no passion for my work. A few months before, I had lost someone extremely important in my life in tragic circumstances.

From the outside, it looked like I was a successful entrepreneur who was living the dream. By most people's standards, I was successful in life and business.

But on the inside, I was miserable. The business, even if it was growing nicely, wasn't fulfilling this new version of myself. Instead, it was slowly burning me out.

At the time of my loss, I had been married for two years. My firstborn daughter was a year old, and I realized that my priorities had shifted. This version of Dave valued family more than scale.

I had to re-align. According to external standards, I was successful, but I wasn't living in alignment with my personal vision. In a move most entrepreneurs would consider crazy, I moved away from a perfectly healthy and thriving business.

I decided to redefine my version of success and think about what really fulfilled me. I came to the realization that gaining fulfillment from your journey is far more valuable than reaching the destination.

**Alignment maximizes your fulfillment
on the road to success.**

Success is the sum of all the steps you take in your journey, plus the happiness you feel when you've completed it. If you love what you do and are aligned with what you truly want, the journey will feel great and always lead you to success. Fulfillment is all about how much enjoyment you get from driving on the road.

You need to evaluate where you are now. When you've done that, you need to make any necessary changes on all levels to ensure you stay in alignment.

We're going to show you how to work with this alignment structure:

Daily > Weekly > Quarterly > Annually > Big Picture

How do you feel at this point in your entrepreneurial journey? Do you feel you're on the right track? Or do you feel that you've drifted? If so, you need to reevaluate your destination and get on another, more fulfilling road.

Creating your Big Picture will help you answer these questions. By the time you've completed the exercise, you'll have set a clear destination. This is your starting point as you embark on a new, successful journey to fulfillment. Let's get started.

The Big Picture
A Snapshot Of Your Success

Imagine that you have met your goals and reached the top of your mountain. While you're up there, you take a moment to look back at the road you've traveled. You reflect on the journey that got you to your destination.

Now imagine that you could take one photo of this moment that you could bring back to your current life and carry with you on your entrepreneurial journey. Just like a father who keeps a photo of his family in his wallet to remind himself what is important in his life, it reminds you where you're going. Completing the Big Picture exercise is like taking that photo.

► Projecting Your Success

I regularly host retreats for entrepreneurs called Business Detox Retreats. The entrepreneurs who come on our retreats have typically drifted far away from their initial vision. They're often exhausted or burned out. They want to disconnect to reconnect with their purpose, and this exercise gives them a framework that helps them set their sights on what they truly want in life.

It also helps them understand the importance of alignment in their life and in their business.

When we give our students this task, we send them to a place of their choosing for two to three hours. On one retreat, I sent them out in nature, in the woods or by the ocean to complete it. When they've finished, I get them to come back in the afternoon so everyone can share their thoughts.

The Big Picture is based on a simple series of questions that I created for myself. It ensures I'm always living a life that's based on my version of success. It's the first part of the alignment process.

It's inspired by an old and classic exercise called "The Perfect Day" or "The Ideal Day." In the traditional version of this exercise, you think about what your perfect average day looks like. But for this edition, we're going to consider a specific day in the future.

You're going to be sitting on top of the mountain and looking at what you've created and witnessed. You'll think about what you've accomplished in your life and business that makes you proud—the things that have impacted you, your family, and your clients.

From there, we're going to do some reverse engineering to work out what you need to do to get there. This exercise is a starting point for your journey. It's a powerful exercise because it highlights your core values. Circumstances change and evolve. However, your core values—who you really are—remain the same.

If you have been roaming the world of entrepreneurship, doing way too much, and losing sight of key goals, this exercise is a way to start reconnecting with them. When we ask people on our retreats to come back after finishing this exercise, and we start sharing as a group, it exposes the gap between what they want and what they're doing. When they have to verbalize and share their big picture with the group, it brings up a lot of strong emotions. It's not rare for us to see experienced entrepreneurs shedding tears. It's a moment they never forget.

For a lot of people, it's a turning point. It makes them realize that what they're doing isn't working for them, and isn't in alignment with what they truly want or what they envision for themselves in the future.

► The 12 Questions You Need To Ask Yourself

There are 12 questions that you need to ask yourself in order to snap a complete picture of your success. You might think this sounds very simple, and in one sense it is. However, the key to this exercise is to do some serious introspection. This will allow you to ask yourself really personal questions without having your mind clouded by someone else's ambitions or vision. We are so easily influenced by so many different people and ideas, especially in this age of social media and an overabundance of online information. We tend to attach ourselves to things we see. It's important to dive deep to find out what you truly want.

To answer these questions. Think about your day from beginning to end. At the end of the day, we're going to celebrate something special.

Here are these questions:

1. What day is it?

First, you need to think of a future date. The time frame is up to you. Some people project themselves 30 years into the future, others only three years from now. Either is fine. It's up to you to choose your destination.

2. Where are you?

Write down where you are. If you have more than one home, specify which one you're staying in.

3. Why is today a special day?

This day is unique because you will celebrate something. What is it? Write down something major that will happen that day.

4. What do you do when you wake up?

Write down when you woke up and the first thing you did. What is your morning routine like? What habits do you have? What is it like?

5. How do you spend your morning, afternoon, and evening?

What activities take up your morning, afternoon, and usual evenings? Be precise with times and how long you spend on each activity. Will you spend time with others, or alone? Your answers will reveal your values, and the type of changes you will need to make before your perfect day can become a reality.

Dream big. You can write about projects you haven't started yet. Even if it will take years for you to begin or complete them, outline what your vision looks like. At the moment, you might still be in the building stage. This exercise isn't about how you're living right now; it's about projecting yourself into the future. Get outside of your comfort zone. Personally, I have a long-term aim to build some business ecosystems. It's not yet on the radar, but it's part of my ultimate vision.

6. What are you happy that you've accomplished?

List a minimum of three of your accomplishments. Remember, you're on top of the mountain, and you're looking back at what you've done. Stay true to your personal style. Your accomplishments should reflect who you are and feel authentic to you.

7. Where does your income come from?

Be specific. What are your income streams? For example, do you make money from one or more businesses, investments, or both? If you own one or more companies, do you take responsibility for the day to day operations, or have you outsourced the work?

8. What are you known for?

List things that you are known for, or want to be remembered for. What would be written on your gravestone? Think about the legacy you want to leave. When your family and friends talk about you, what would you like them to say?

9. What are you fortunate to have?

Write down what you have and own. You could list material possessions or investments. You could also list less tangible but still valuable things like your health, relationships, and time to create meaningful, impactful projects. Don't forget about the important things you are able to do on a daily basis that fills you with a sense of gratitude.

10. Out of everything, what's the one thing you're the most proud of?

This could be anything; it could be business-related, something personal or both.

11. What have you been able to experience personally?

Think of this as scratched items on your bucket list. If you like to travel, write down where you like to go. They could be places you already know you like or places you have yet to explore. This part of the exercise helps you think about the kind of experiences you want to be a part of. Most people say they'd like to do something "one day," but that's too vague. This exercise helps bring your aspirations into focus. In time, you might be able to narrow your ideal location down from countries to regions or towns.

List three things that you want to see or witness. These experiences could be related to travel, hobbies, major sporting events, experiences you want to share with family or friends, or anything else that really matters to you. Again, allow yourself to dream big.

12. Who will be there at the celebration and how will you celebrate?

List the people you are with. Who do you want to be there as you celebrate this special event? It could be people in your life now, or people you don't know yet. They could be people you want to make friends with in the future; perhaps they are people you look up to. Who do you want to attract into your life that will be important for you in your journey? How does this great day end? While the celebration is going on, what will YOU do specifically to celebrate?

► Your Big Picture May Change Over Time

As we get older, our goals, priorities, and worldview change. Your 20-year-old and 40-year-old selves want different things. That's perfectly okay. It's never too late to amend your vision and reset your destination.

Your vision is based on a mix of timeless principles and current values that will evolve over time based on experience and personal context. Every year will bring a new and unpredictable set of events, and you'll need to adjust your vision accordingly.

I recommend redoing your Big Picture once a year. Personally, I do it during my macro Business Detox that I schedule for the end of every year. It's a great way to check that I'm headed on the right path to achieving what I want in my professional and personal life.

► Big Picture Example

I review my Big Picture every year because my circumstances always change. Sometimes, as my vision gets closer, I gain more clarity about what I specifically want. Other times, I realize that my Big Picture from the previous year was a little off track. It happens. But it's never too late to correct the course.

To give you an example, here's what my Big Picture looks like:

Tonight is August 21st, 2032.

I am here at my house in Nova Scotia, Canada, on our private island (summer cottage). Today is a special day because I am celebrating my 50th birthday.

This morning I woke up at 5:00 A.M. to the sound of crashing waves. I had water and coffee, and journaled while watching the sunrise from our private beach, sitting on an Adirondack chair. I then did a 30-minute workout followed by a 30-minute walk. I grabbed fresh eggs from our farm on my way back to the cottage and had a great breakfast on the patio with my wife Karine and our two daughters.

After breakfast, I had my daily huddle with Cedric, my right-hand man for the past 17 years. It was followed by a 2-hour block to complete my daily tasks and work routines. I'm now completely removed from the "doing" in my companies, but I am still very present.

Early in the afternoon, I went fly fishing. I caught a beautiful Atlantic wild salmon that we'll eat tomorrow. At 3 P.M. I had coffee with one of our investors who lives on the mainland, in the entrepreneurs' community we built around our island.

After coffee and a great talk, I took my boat to get back on our island.

Today, I have to get ready for tonight's celebration, but on a regular day, we always cook dinner together as a family and then take it easy for the rest of the evening. We usually try to keep it open.

I'm able to live like this now because over the past years we have:

- *Transformed the lives of hundreds of thousands of entrepreneurs with Effic, and the company is now world-renowned in the business leadership development world, selling more than 1,000,000 copies of the Effic Planner, and it is now available in multiple languages. We also have Effic Certified Partners in more than 50 countries.*

- *Assembled and empowered a great team that takes care of running my businesses without me having to be there all the time.*

- *Build a global network of world-changing leader friends to create five entrepreneurial communities around the world in which we develop business ecosystems that work together on some of the world's biggest sustainability challenges in various fields.*

Now my income comes from the businesses that I founded and that are now self-driving. We also have revenue coming from our diversified investments portfolio.

I am known for being a man with high standards for himself, his family life, and his health. I'm appreciated for my loyalty, my epicurean side, and my passion for helping others succeed. I'm respected for my sense of community and desire to see the world thrive in a sustainable way.

I'm fortunate to now have remarkable health, I'm grateful to have access to fresh food directly from the source and for still being able to play hockey at least twice a week without feeling like the old man on the ice. I'm also grateful for my two very smart, curious, and ambitious daughters. I'm also grateful to have unplanned lunch and dinner dates with Karine regularly.

I'm thankful to have a lot of time and space to work on projects that have a great impact. We also have generational wealth that I want my kids and grandkids to use to create great things. On a lighter note, I'm also proud of my collection of whiskeys and cigars, as well as my Montreal Canadiens memorabilia.

But what makes me proudest is my 20-year marriage to Karine, who has been, by far, the best thing to ever happen to me.

All this allowed us to:

- *Travel regularly outside of Canada, mostly to the Caribbeans, New Zealand, Iceland, and Patagonia, where our communities are located. We have a private house in each place.*
- *Spend four days at Francis Malmann's private island for an epicurean adventure where he shared his secrets to wild open fire cooking.*
- *Be at the Bell Center when the Montreal Canadiens won their 25th Stanley Cup.*

Tonight, I am here with my wife Karine, our two daughters, our parents, brothers, and sisters. Our best friends also flew in from all over the world to celebrate with us.

We'll have a big feast, dance and share stories around a big camp-
fire. This is my favorite way to celebrate. I'm also going to treat
myself and our guests by opening a bottle of 50-year old Japanese
whiskey and sharing a box of rare Cuban cigars from my humidor.

Every year, when I do this exercise, I evaluate the strength of my desire to see this Big Picture become a reality. The great news so far is that I feel like I'm getting closer and closer to it. The bad news, as I'm writing these lines, is that the Montreal Canadiens still haven't won their 25th Stanley Cup (Go Habs Go!).

But the main point here is the value of having dreams. It doesn't matter if your dream doesn't turn out exactly the way you imagined; the value is who you become in its pursuit.

The Annual Guideline
Your Objectives For The Next 12 Months

As a multibillionaire investor with a phenomenal track record, Warren Buffett is among the most financially successful people who have ever lived. He's also something of a curiosity in the business world. Instead of frantically working all hours, he takes a decidedly minimalist approach to his schedule, preferring to delegate as many tasks as possible and focusing his attention only on what matters most to him.

What's his secret? How does he decide where to channel his time and energy? Simple—he knows how to pick goals that align with his vision.

The Story Of Mike Flint

Mike Flint flew Buffett around the globe for ten years as his personal pilot. One day, as they were flying, Flint told Buffet that he wanted more to life; that he felt as though he still had a long way to go when it came to his own goals.

Buffett shared his wisdom with him. He gave him a three-step exercise that would change the pilot's life. It can change yours too!

Step 1: Buffett asked Flint to make a list of his top 25 goals. These could be both Flint's personal and professional life. Flint took some time to think about them and wrote his goals down. He felt that they were representative of his personal view of success.

Step 2: Buffet then asked Flint to make some tough choices. Buffett told him to narrow his list of 25 goals down by circling only the five goals that held the most significance for him. After reflection, Flint made five circles. Buffet then asked Flint, *"Are you sure these are the absolute highest priority for you?"* Flint nodded his head confidently.

Step 3: At this point, Flint had two lists: List A that was made of the five circled items and List B with the 20 other items remaining.

Flint assured Buffett that these goals were so meaningful to him that he'd start working towards them that very evening. He knew how he'd achieve them. He knew the steps he needed to take. He even knew who he would ask for help.

But Buffett then asked Flint a big question:

"What about these other 20 things on your list that you didn't circle?"

Flint explained that he would work on his other 20 goals when he could find the time in between focusing on his top 5 goals. After all, he still valued the goals on "List B."

Buffett then imparted his sage advice: *"No. You've got it wrong, Mike,"* he said. *"Everything you didn't circle just became your 'avoid at all cost' list. No matter what, these things get no attention from you until you've succeeded with your top 5."*

The lesson was clear. If Flint wanted to succeed at anything, he had to learn to direct his time, energy, and attention towards the goals that mattered most. He had to fight the temptation to try achieving everything at once.

With the Effic method, we take the same approach. If you have too many goals on your list, you are setting yourself up to fail. Five isn't the magic number when it comes to goals, but sticking to it as an upper limit will help you focus. You can choose to concentrate on fewer than five goals, but don't chase more than that at any one time.

However tempting it may be to set yourself more than 5, resist the urge. Have you ever tried going to the grocery store to buy a lot of items without a list? Don't try it. I can guarantee that when you unpack your groceries at home, you'll have forgotten many of the things you set out to buy. The same principle applies here. Sticking to a small number of goals will keep you on track.

► The Importance Of Strategic Alignment

The fastest way to get anywhere is in a straight line, and strategic alignment will guide you along your journey. Your five goals—that is, your points of focus—will become your Annual Guideline. The name is self-explanatory. Drawing up an Annual Guideline will help you determine the most important things that you're going to focus on over the coming year.

Ask yourself these questions: "What do I want to see become a reality in my life or business over the next 12 months?" and "What do I really want to manifest within the coming year?" Your answers will determine your goals and your Annual Guideline.

The Annual Guideline forms the groundwork for all the other strategies and systems in this book. With that in mind, I would strongly advise that you try your best to be as thorough as possible when performing the following exercise. Your answers will shape your entire year in terms of projection and planning.

Your Annual Guideline should always be aligned with your Big Picture.

A simple way to ensure your five annual objectives are right is to ask yourself this question for each item: "Is this in line with my Big Picture?"

If the answer is "Yes," you're on the right path. If the answer is "No, but…" you need to reconsider this goal.

The same goes for any projects you take on quarterly, the time you invest weekly or tasks you perform daily, ask yourself this question: "Is this in line with my Annual Guideline?"

The Annual Guideline will always keep you on the right path. It is a compass that gives you the directions you need to follow your magnetic north in a straight line. Committing to being in alignment will give you the results you want.

► Don't Let FOMO Make You Drift

The process of drawing up your Annual Guideline is tough. You'll probably feel cornered, especially if you feel like everything on your list is important. But this is a good thing, as it forces you to listen carefully to your instincts. In order for this exercise to work properly, you have to reduce your list to a total of 5 key goals.

There's no need to worry about "Fear Of Missing Out" (FOMO). You'll have plenty of opportunities to reassess your Annual Guideline later and realign yourself if necessary. In fact, your alignment is a dynamic process; you'll have to keep it in check regularly. We'll look at this in greater depth later in the book.

Do not keep both lists. Ditch List B. You want to create a Guideline that lets you focus. Anything else beyond the Guideline is just a distraction. You're going to put those other 20 goals aside. The five objectives you circled on your original list are those you care about the most. Think about it. So, by definition, the rest automatically become nothing but distractions.

► Why Your Guideline Items Should Be Outcomes, Not Projects

Your goals need to be quantifiable, with a specific outcome attached to each. A set of goals usually reflect both personal and professional aspirations. Earlier in this book, we talked about the principle of Life & Business Harmony. Life and business are always interconnected, and your goals will shape you on both a personal and professional level. You don't need to have a particular project in mind when setting a goal or measuring its results.

I often see people trying to use their Annual Guideline as a list of projects that they want to accomplish over the course of a year. They then try to break them down into subgoals. This is a big mistake; it's not how the Annual Guideline should be used. The ProductivAction process will take care of planning and compiling a list of projects, and we'll cover it later in this book. For now, just take some time to focus on your goals. The items in your Annual Guideline are likely to be project outcomes but not necessarily the projects themselves.

Let's look at an example. Here's what your reduced list could look like:

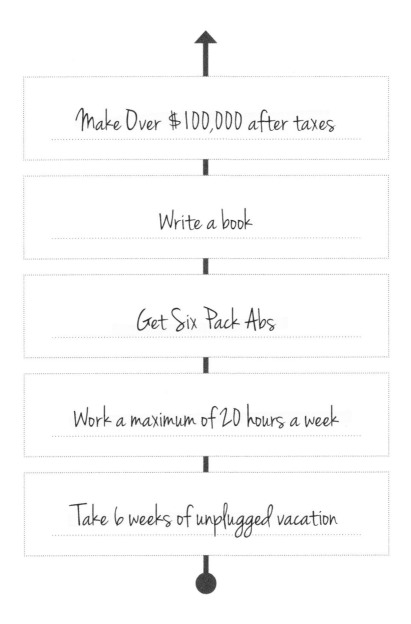

Make Over $100,000 after taxes

Write a book

Get Six Pack Abs

Work a maximum of 20 hours a week

Take 6 weeks of unplugged vacation

These goals are all quantifiable. Twelve months from now, it will be clear whether you've achieved them or not.

The journey ahead is long. It will take a lot of time and effort to scale your personal mountain and meet your goals.

Most people have dreams, but they never draw up a strategy that will get them to their destination. The Annual Guideline is your first step. When used correctly, it will ensure you are aligned at all times. This will keep you focused.

Keep in mind that this guideline, just like your Big Picture, will evolve to adapt to changes in your context. It will also require frequent alignment checks and opportunities to realign if needed. As you'll see later, you'll have multiple opportunities to evaluate your Guideline to ensure alignment.

You've now set your focus for the year. You've picked a direction. Now all you have to do is take action without drifting. For this, you'll need to learn the art of careful prioritization. In the next part, you'll learn how to master this skill.

Step Two

Prioritization

effic

Every waking moment, we are all making choices about how to use our time. Are you making the most of yours?

The unfortunate truth is that all too often, we spend time on things that aren't important.

To make better decisions, we need to prioritize. Prioritization is the art of identifying what actually matters. It's about making the right choices. People who know how to prioritize items on their to-do lists don't cram their schedules with as many tasks as possible. Instead, they know the value of picking the right tasks and executing them. They put quality over quantity.

Prioritization is essential for proper alignment. It stops you from losing sight of the things you really want and wasting time on things that don't matter. It prevents you from getting bogged down by reactivity. As entrepreneurs, we are easily distracted. By getting your priorities in order, you'll stay on the right road and won't fall into the trap of trying to do too many things at once.

Prioritization follows naturally from the Projection step because once you know what you want, it's easier to decide how to invest your time, energy, and attention in order to get it. During the Prioritization step, you'll identify the Power Moves that will move the needle in your business.

By now, you know where you're going. You've established your big picture. You've created your annual guideline, and drafted the five major goals you're going to hit within the next 12 months.

But now that you've outlined your goals and objectives, you might be starting to worry that you'll fall into old patterns and bad habits. You may be wondering how to stay on course and remain strategically productive instead of lurching randomly from one task to the next.

To overcome this problem, you'll need to begin by prioritizing two essential tasks that are guaranteed to yield high-impact results in your business.

The Impact Matrix

*How To Prioritize Efficiently To
Double Your Productivity*

A big mistake that most entrepreneurs make is to operate from a position of reactivity. They know what they need to do to move the needle in their business, but because they are in a reactive state of management, new items keep adding to their do-list. They carry out the day to day operations that keep their business going, but the pile-up of tasks that never get done continues to grow. This is why many projects that would help the company grow never see the light of day.

Fortunately, there's a solution. In this chapter, we're going to use a tool called the Impact Matrix. You'll learn that there are four different types of tasks. Each is distinguishable by its nature, impact, and energetic cost. By focusing on the right tasks, you'll enjoy better growth and learn to work more efficiently.

► The Eisenhower Matrix Problem

You've probably heard of the Eisenhower Matrix. It's very popular with productivity and business coaches. As shown in the diagram below, the matrix provides a template for assessing tasks according to their urgency and importance. The idea is that when you have completed the matrix, you'll know when you should do each task.

- *Urgent, Important* tasks should be completed immediately.
- *Urgent, Not Important* tasks should be delegated to other people.
- *Not Urgent, Important* tasks should be scheduled to ensure they are done, but they don't have to be completed in the immediate future.
- *Not Urgent, Not Important* tasks should be eliminated.

However, the matrix has serious limitations, at least in a business context. To appreciate why, you need to understand its origins.

The matrix is named after US army general Dwight David Eisenhower, who served during World War II and was elected President from 1953 to 1961. Eisenhower once declared that he faced two kinds of problems: urgent problems and important problems. As someone who built his career in the military, Eisenhower's approach to task management was developed in a military context during wartime, where responsiveness and reactivity were vital. It made sense for him to classify tasks along these two dimensions because his job entailed making a series of rapid high-stakes decisions.

This method worked well for Eisenhower, and the matrix still holds a lot of appeal today. Unfortunately, it doesn't work in the context of our Effic philosophy.

There's nothing wrong with classifying tasks using the matrix. The problem is that qualifying these tasks isn't as straight-forward as we're led to believe. How do you know which tasks are important? And how do you gauge the urgency of a task?

In my experience, the majority of entrepreneurs who try to use this matrix end up putting most of the tasks in the top left box. They end up exactly where they started—with a humongous to-do list that leaves them feeling overwhelmed. Most entrepreneurs who lose their freedom operate from a responsive and reactive standpoint. Everything feels urgent, and they go through tasks on a "first come, first serve" basis.

	URGENT	NOT URGENT
IMPORTANT	DO IT NOW	SCHEDULE IT
NOT IMPORTANT	DELEGATE	DELETE

Priorities Change Because We Prioritize Urgency

According to the matrix, tasks classified as *important but not urgent* need to be scheduled. However, do you currently have space for scheduling new tasks? Most entrepreneurs don't. But don't worry! Later in this book, we'll fix this by showing you how to put together an effective task schedule using the Done By Noon framework.

Schedule space isn't the only issue. Most entrepreneurs struggle with delegating the *urgent but not important* tasks. Without a proper system to channel these new tasks, they can quickly turn into fire accelerators, making the overwhelm entirely out of control. When you always feel under fire, you'll more than often take ownership of these tasks, putting them back into the "urgent and important" bucket. It happens to all entrepreneurs. No one's teaching you this before you start your business. Delegating isn't easy nor natural for most of us. It's a big game of figuring things out that we all have to play at one point in our careers. Fortunately, we have an excellent system to help you with this.

What about deleting tasks? Although it sounds appealing, eliminating tasks can be a bad idea. Some entrepreneurs delete tasks because they don't want to do them and don't have good delegation skills. They end up putting things that don't hold their interest in the "not urgent and not important" bucket. But in avoiding these inconvenient "details" or "minor tasks," they are headed for disaster.

Given all these limitations, it's no wonder that the Eisenhower matrix is often abused. Let me show you how to create a matrix that uses more appropriate axes.

► Impact vs. Effort

In order to categorize tasks, we use what we call the Impact Matrix. To use it effectively, you need to understand that there are four types of tasks. Some are more important than others, but we measure them all along two axes: impact and effort.

The effort axis runs along the bottom of the chart. This axis allows you to identify the amount of effort you need to provide to complete the task successfully. We work from an efficiency standpoint, so good energy management is key to making this process work.

The vertical axis measures impact. The more important a task is to the running and development of your business, the higher its impact. Completing high-impact tasks needs to become a top priority. If you only do tasks that have minimal impact, how do you expect your business to grow and reach its goals?

THE EFFIC® IMPACT MATRIX

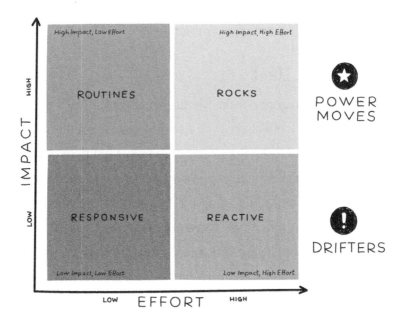

► The 4 Types Of Work Tasks

ROUTINES High Impact, Low effort

These are recurring tasks that are necessary for the proper functioning of your business.

You have to keep performing them on a regular basis—for example, every day or every week—to ensure that everything is running smoothly. The tasks are high-impact because they are needed for the general health and financial success of your ventures. Without them, you'll soon go under.

However, although they are important, they are also low-effort. We have adapted to these tasks. You've performed them many times before, and you're comfortable with the process.

When you adapt to an exercise, it gets easier to perform the more often you repeat it. The same principle applies here. Whether on a conscious or unconscious level, it's likely you've adopted procedures that help you get these tasks done quickly and efficiently.

Examples of routine tasks:

- Paying invoices
- Prospecting new clients
- Social media posting as part of a content marketing strategy
- Bookkeeping

ROCKS High Impact, High Effort

These are tasks associated with projects and innovation.

Businesses need to innovate if they are to grow. Tapping into our creative powers is one of the most exciting parts of being an entrepreneur. But how many times have you postponed a project because you just didn't have time to work on it? The sad truth is that lots of entrepreneurs are not going to see their businesses grow because they are too busy to do tasks that are both urgent and important.

That's where Rocks come in. By identifying and managing them, you'll have time to do whatever it takes to move your business to the next level. Rocks are tasks that underpin specific projects or innovations. They are high-impact because they help you create new products and services. They open up new financial avenues that generate more income. Rocks are also high-effort tasks. Compared to Routines, they require more energy and demand your best performance.

These two types of tasks—Routines and Rocks—are your **Power Moves.** When it comes to investing your time, they yield the best results. To grow your business, you need to prioritize them in your schedule. I'm going to show you exactly how to do this later in this book.

Now, let's look at the second tier of tasks. These are tasks that are directly related to how you manage your business.

RESPONSIVE Low Impact, Low Effort

These are tasks associated with impromptu interpersonal communication such as emails, unplanned meetings, calls, texts, and direct messages.

If you aren't prepared to deal with these kinds of tasks in an efficient manner, they will eat up many hours of your time.

For example, if you decide to reply to messages on an "as and when" basis, you could end up swapping trivial messages with an associate or colleague for half an hour when one simple, well-structured email would have done the job. Or, if you agree to an unplanned meeting, you could spend an afternoon discussing interesting but irrelevant ideas that do nothing to move you closer to your goals.

Responsive tasks are low-effort and low-impact, but they are still mandatory for the running of your business. Unlike Routines, they don't have a significant impact on your financial success. However, they still need to be accounted for and scheduled.

If you're not careful, these tasks can soon get out of control and eat up hours of your precious time. Conversational tasks associated with interpersonal communication, such as emails, meetings, and calls, fit into this category.

Of course, it's essential to communicate with colleagues, customers, and employees. But consider how these tasks sap your energy and fill up your schedule. For example, take email management. Many companies—even large businesses—sacrifice their productivity because they operate from their inboxes. Or consider meetings. Many are poorly planned; in fact, they are often a complete waste of effort.

You can't eliminate these tasks, but you can use a system to ensure they are done quickly and efficiently. The Done By Noon framework will help you schedule your communications and draw up boundaries that limit the time you spend on them. For now, it's important to understand that Responsive tasks can soon overwhelm you if not handled carefully.

REACTIVE Low Impact, High Effort

These tasks are often unplanned and resulting from your day to day activities and operations of your business.

If you add more items to your to-do list every week than you tick off, you're probably dealing with too many Reactive tasks.

No matter what kind of business you run, you'll come up against Reactive tasks. Plans change, new opportunities appear, and obstacles arise. That's inevitable. However, it's all too easy to get sucked into reacting to these developments. Many people end up spending a lot of time doing the things that they feel they should be doing right now, even though many of these tasks can wait. We tend to label them as important and urgent incorrectly.

As your business grows, you'll take on more responsibilities. You'll get busier, and these tasks will begin piling up. If you aren't careful, you'll spend most of your time on this busy-work, at the cost of your energy. We call Responsive tasks and Reactive tasks **Drifters**. Together, these are secondary tasks that will contribute the most to the drift and will eventually get you lost in a lengthy, unmanageable to-do list.

► How To Put The Impact Matrix Into Action

Remember: Not all tasks are created equal. They don't all carry the same weight, both in terms of impact generated and effort required. That being said, you can't neglect any of them. The Drifters, when handled properly, won't actually make you drift. But, if you keep prioritizing them above everything else, always labeling them as important and urgent, I can guarantee that you will pivot off course. On the other hand, the Power Moves—when approached the right way—will have an incredibly positive effect on your freedom!

Here is how you should go about using the Impact Matrix:

1. **Make An Inventory Of Your Tasks**

Make a list of the tasks you perform over the course of a week and put them into one of the four categories in the matrix.

For example, bookkeeping is classified as a routine. You need to do it on a regular basis, whatever type of business you run.

For each task, evaluate how much energy it takes for you to perform. Look how close the task is to your genius and good zones, as shown earlier in the book.

2. Create Rocks and Fill Your Buckets

We'll introduce you to the ProductivAction process in the next chapter. It will show you how to break down your projects into bite-sized pieces, gauge the workload associated with each project, and how to use "buckets" to reach your goals without being overloaded.

3. Document Routines and Apply Leverage

You'll need to standardize your recurring tasks by documenting them and creating procedures. We'll cover this in greater detail later. As you'll go through this process, the rule of thumb is to gradually Delegate, Outsource, or Automate (D.O.A.) the tasks that aren't within reach of your superpowers.

4. Channel Reactive Tasks using "FIONA's Desk"

Many years ago, to deal with the increasing number of daily new tasks caused by the rapid growth of one of our companies, we developed a system called "FIONA's Desk." FIONA stands for Figure It Out and Next Action.

This is a basic protocol that we all have to use when an unplanned task appears. Here it is:

a. Ask yourself: Can we wait until next Monday to plan this task? More often than not, the answer is "Yes." If it's really urgent and important, we act on it. However, this is the exception, not the rule.

b. If it can wait until next Monday when we have our weekly team meeting, we put it on FIONA's desk. FIONA isn't just an acronym. We treat her as a member of the team. We picture her as an angry old woman who doesn't like to have other people touching things on her desk. If you do, she will yell at you. She might even start a fight. However, she will allow you to go through her desk once a week. At that point, you can engage with the task again.

c. Each Monday, we review the tasks on FIONA's desk and put them on our to-do list of secondary tasks, and it is delegated to the right person on the team.

It's a simple system that pays great dividends. It keeps us focused and prevents drift, ensuring we stay on track and reach our goals.

5. **Control Your Responsive Input**

Prioritizing urgency is the quickest way to kill your freedom and fill your schedule with Drifters.

Allowing Responsive tasks to take priority can have extremely negative consequences, not only on your focus but also on your health.

If you open the door to these tasks, your brain will switch into an anxious, responsive mode, paying attention to these tasks at the cost of everything else. You must understand that these tasks can quickly get you out of control and need to be contained.

This is the main reason why I don't encourage the use of chats as the main source of communication within teams. By their very nature, chats force you to be responsive. They are made for conversations. When you're in a chat, and you're not available to answer a message quickly, you get stressed. You worry about the potential consequences of missing a crucial part of the conversation, even if the only thing you risk missing out on are some memes from Sally in Accounting.

What about email for internal communications? Compared to live chat, email doesn't require you to be as responsive, but it's not a great alternative. It soon gets messy when more than two people are involved.

By the way, if you look in the Additional Resources section, you'll find a link to our tried and tested Inbox Freedom System. This A-to-Z, step-by-step framework will show you exactly how to achieve "inbox zero" every single day.

Proper communication is key to running your business. You will need to attend planned meetings and have ongoing conversations with your customers, employees, and colleagues. However, communication should always be part of a proactive routine. It should never be responsive.

In our business, we use an asynchronous platform for internal communication. It forces us to be proactive and plan ahead instead of figuring things out on the fly. We do use live chat very occasionally, but only to deal with urgent and important matters, which doesn't happen often.

The Done By Noon framework will show you how to schedule communication-based tasks. Depending on the needs of your business, you might schedule them on a daily or weekly basis. Optimizing communication will help you avoid Responsive tasks and reduce the number of Reactive tasks. Ultimately, your communications will become more meaningful and impactful.

We've covered a lot of ground in this chapter, but here's the bottom line: always prioritize your Power Moves. These high-impact tasks will propel your business forward and lay the foundations of your success. In the next chapter, I'll show you how to optimize them and make the best possible use of your time.

PowerMove #1: Rocks

*How To Break Down Your Projects
Into Bite-Size Actions Using The
ProductivAction™ Process*

In this chapter, we're going to consider how you should prioritize your project-based tasks. Your major challenge here is to identify and organize them.

As entrepreneurs, we have the gift of creativity. We use this creativity to devise the solutions we offer the world in the form of products and services. An entrepreneur is never short of ideas and visions, and these lay the foundations for our projects.

However, to enjoy real freedom, you need to embrace a healthy structure that will help you unleash your creativity and consistently materialize ideas and projects. When most people think of a creative person, they imagine a free spirit with no boundaries. In fact, the most creative people in the world have a well-structured creative process. This is what the Productivation Process offers you as an entrepreneur.

► The Pickle Jar Theory Workout

Dr. Stephen Covey, the author of the bestselling book *The Seven Habits Of Highly Effective People,* popularized this theory in the '80s. He liked to use this powerful metaphor to illustrate why prioritization is the key to achieving your goals.

I'll always remember the first time I saw his demo: Covey pulled a jar out from under a table, along with big rocks, smaller rocks, and some sand.

He started pouring sand into the jar, followed by the small rocks, and then the big rocks. Everyone watching knew that it would be impossible to fit everything in the jar. With a layer of sand at the bottom and the small rocks on top, there was no room left for the big rocks.

Covey went through the demonstration again, but this time he took a different approach. He began by putting the big rocks into the jar. Then he added the small rocks. Finally, he poured in the sand. Using this method, he could easily fit everything into the jar. The small rocks fit into the gaps between the large rocks, and the sand filled the remaining space when all the rocks had been added.

What Covey exposed here is that in our personal and professional lives, we have big rocks, small rocks, and sand. The natural tendency is to give priority to sand, leaving little room for rocks. We spend most of our lives taking care of small tasks and neglecting the important ones.

We must get our priorities in order if we want to create space in our lives. This is a powerful lesson. But what was even more powerful was the big "Aha moment" I had after hearing this story. I connected the dots and saw that the ideas underlying this metaphor mapped precisely onto the principles of load management and periodization. This is the same type of framework I used to design my programs.

When you create a workout program, you need to create goal specific sets. You must choose the right exercises and break your workout down into sets and reps. I realized that structuring a workout was similar to fitting big rocks, small rocks, and sand in a jar. All the components have to be carefully planned and arranged, or it won't yield the right results.

I immediately understood that if I wanted a project to come to life, I needed to apply the same principle. Most entrepreneurs make the mistake of prioritizing sand. That's why so many of their projects never come to fruition. We tend to prioritize the small stuff. We get caught up in day-to-day details instead of working on what will truly move our businesses forward. Ultimately there is just too much sand in the jar. It overflows, and the load becomes too heavy to carry. Having read the chapter on load management, this idea should resonate with you.

I also started to integrate the concept of creating space into my approach. Consider this: When you think you don't have enough space, as shown in the overflowing jar above, you have two options:

1. You can get a bigger jar, thereby increasing the amount of space you have at your disposal, which will increase the load.
2. You can learn to prioritize. This will let you place the rocks in the jar in the right order so that they will fit.

When you choose the second option, something magical happens—you'll create space! Space is one of the key pillars of entrepreneurial freedom.

I embarked on a mission to apply these insights and build a productive project management process to reclaim my creative freedom. I named this process ProductivAction, a name that stays true to the "Working Right" approach to productivity. It's all about achieving the right results. To do that, you need to identify the right actions that will give you these results. Every action matters because each one moves you closer to your goal.

► The ProductivAction™ Process

Just as you need to prepare when you begin a workout program, you need to set aside time to get ready before starting a project.

Picture this. Imagine that in front of you, I've placed three buckets with big rocks and small rocks.

Your bucket represents a project. I prefer the term "bucket" to "jar." A bucket works better for carrying objects around, so it's more effective when illustrating load management. Your big rocks represent milestones, which are the key steps to complete your project. The small rocks represent bite-sized actions known as ProductivActions, or P.A. for short.

SAND

SMALL ROCKS

BIG ROCKS

BUCKET

Let me explain the three-step process you will need to break down your projects into milestones and actions. The template you'll see below is extracted from the Effic Planner. You'll find a link to a printable version in the additional resources section at the end of the book.

Step 1: Label Your Buckets For The Next Quarter

With our methodology, you have a maximum of three buckets available per quarter, representing a total of three projects. The number of buckets you will use is up to you, but three is the maximum number you should try to carry. Give each bucket a label that describes your project.

Why is three buckets the limit? The answer is simple. It comes back to load management. We've established that three buckets is the maximum workload someone can personally carry on a quarterly basis. Don't be fooled, three full buckets will be heavy to carry. The truth is that the load you'll be able to carry depends on your current capacity.

Here, we're going to use the project example of an online training course. This quarter, you want to create a new video-based online training course. You establish that you'd need three buckets to complete this project. The three buckets are then labeled:

1. "Course Design" where you'll create the core marketing, course curriculum, branding, and support material.

2. "Videos For Online Course" where you'll produce the videos for the course.

3. "Online Course Launch" where you'll create the final marketing material, launch and start selling your course to your audience

This is a good example of a multi-bucket project here. To continue the case study, we'll use the example of your second bucket: "Videos For Online Course" and show you in detail how this bucket can be filled.

Videos For Online Course

MILESTONE (BIG ROCK):

☐ ....

TO COMPLETE BY:

....

ACTIONS (SMALL ROCKS):

☐ ....

☐ ....

☐ ....

☐ ....

☐ ....

MILESTONE (BIG ROCK):

☐ ....

TO COMPLETE BY:

....

ACTIONS (SMALL ROCKS):

☐ ....

☐ ....

☐ ....

☐ ....

☐ ....

MILESTONE (BIG ROCK):

☐ ....

TO COMPLETE BY:

....

ACTIONS (SMALL ROCKS):

☐ ....

☐ ....

☐ ....

☐ ....

☐ ....

MILESTONE (BIG ROCK):

☐ ....

TO COMPLETE BY:

....

ACTIONS (SMALL ROCKS):

☐ ....

☐ ....

☐ ....

☐ ....

☐ ....

Step 2: Fill Each Bucket With A Maximum Of Four Big Rocks

You're now going to fill each bucket with a maximum of four big rocks. These big rocks represent the milestones that you must accomplish for this project.

Identifying your four big rocks will be difficult at first. You'll probably ask yourself, "How do I know what my big rocks are?" To answer this question, you will need to start thinking strategically by reverse engineering your projects.

Something you will realize when you use this process is that some projects are actually bigger than you first imagined. Sometimes a project will require two or even three buckets. That means a big project can potentially be three back to back projects, meaning it will be made of up to 12 big rocks. Remember, the bucket is a metaphor for your workload. It is pointless to overfill your bucket and try to make all the rocks fit in it. That's a quick path to exhaustion.

Your four milestones could be named:

- Pre-production
- Production
- Post-production
- Upload on course platform

For each milestone, it's preferable that you set a due date for it.

Videos For Online Course

MILESTONE (BIG ROCK):
☐ Pre-Production

TO COMPLETE BY:
January 20th

ACTIONS (SMALL ROCKS):
☐
☐
☐
☐
☐

MILESTONE (BIG ROCK):
☐ Production

TO COMPLETE BY:
February 20th

ACTIONS (SMALL ROCKS):
☐
☐
☐
☐
☐

MILESTONE (BIG ROCK):
☐ Post-Production

TO COMPLETE BY:
March 15th

ACTIONS (SMALL ROCKS):
☐
☐
☐
☐
☐

MILESTONE (BIG ROCK):
☐ Upload On Course Platform

TO COMPLETE BY:
March 31st

ACTIONS (SMALL ROCKS):
☐
☐
☐
☐
☐

Step 3: Break Down Each Big Rock Into No More Than Five Small Rocks

Once we've established what the big rocks are, it's time to break them down into smaller ones. The third step is to break down each big rock into a maximum of five small rocks. Ask yourself, "What are the steps I need to take in order to reach each milestone?" You may discover that a project is made up of more small rocks than you anticipated. That's OK. It simply means that your big rock is larger than you had envisaged. To make it more manageable, it can be made into two separate big rocks.

It takes practice to master this process. With time, you'll begin to see commonalities between projects. When it's time to start a project, your brain will automatically start applying this framework. You'll gain more self-awareness; you'll have greater insight into the kind of load you can manage, as well as the type of load required to complete a project. This is a crucial step on your journey to becoming a more sustainably performant entrepreneur.

For example, for the big rock "Pre-Production," the five small rocks would be:

1. Find a shooting location
2. Book filming location
3. Find the equipment
4. Create a storyboard for each video
5. Pick 5 outfits

Here's what it looks like once all filled:

Videos For Online Course

MILESTONE (BIG ROCK):
☐ Pre-Production

TO COMPLETE BY:
January 20th

ACTIONS (SMALL ROCKS):
☐ Find a shooting location
☐ Book filming location
☐ Find the equipment
☐ Create a storyboard for each video
☐ Pick 5 outfits

MILESTONE (BIG ROCK):
☐ Production

TO COMPLETE BY:
February 10th

ACTIONS (SMALL ROCKS):
☐ Set lighting
☐ Sound test
☐ 2 Camera setting
☐ Backup on hard drives
☐

MILESTONE (BIG ROCK):
☐ Post-Production

TO COMPLETE BY:
February 28th

ACTIONS (SMALL ROCKS):
☐ Editing
☐ Add Subtitles
☐ Insert Slides
☐ Music
☐ Rendering

MILESTONE (BIG ROCK):
☐ Upload On Course Platform

TO COMPLETE BY:
March 31st

ACTIONS (SMALL ROCKS):
☐ Create all course parts on platform
☐ Upload videos on server
☐ Set download link for each video
☐
☐

> Download the **ProductivAction Bucket** template at
www.DoneByNoonBook.com/Toolbox

► Key Points

As you go through this process, there are several key points you must bear in mind.

1. **Remember that you will be working on each project (i.e., each bucket) for 90 days at a time.** In sports performance words, these will be your mesocycles.

2. **You should not have more than three buckets to carry.** Remember the principle of load management. You need to understand the load that you can carry if you want to perform to your full potential and stay productive. If your buckets are too heavy, your situation is not sustainable. You won't be able to reach your goals within the time frame you established. You don't have to start with three buckets right away. In fact, it's best to do one or two buckets to get started as you develop your understanding of this approach. You'll soon improve, and your capacity will increase.

3. **It might take a few cycles to adapt to this method.** It's going to take you two to three quarters to master this approach. But eventually, whenever you see a project or opportunity, your brain is going to start thinking in terms of the big rocks, small rocks, and sand that would make up the project. You'll start thinking about deadlines, and begin asking yourself, "OK, how can I achieve these milestones? What steps do I need to take?"

4. **You need to stay aligned with your Annual Guideline.** Always ask yourself, "Is this project in line with what I want to achieve in the next 90 days? Is this in line with what I want to do?" Be honest with yourself. Is each project going to help you get there?

5. **Don't think about the sand for now.** The sand represents the microtasks that you'll need to accomplish each action. They are important, but now is not the time to plan them. If you focus on the sand at this stage, you'll be overplanning, which is worse than underplanning. You'll get sucked into the sand and small details, and you won't accomplish anything. Stay focused on the rocks.

PowerMove #2: Routines
How To Turn Repetitive And Recurring
Tasks Into Leveraged Processes

In business, a vast majority of your operations consist of tasks that must be completed on a daily, weekly, monthly, or yearly basis to ensure that it runs smoothly.

Most of them are easy to perform; you've done them many times. These tasks are so easy that we don't even think about optimizing them, and maybe you don't even schedule them. These tasks have such a low energetic cost that you don't account for them when planning your workload.

Unfortunately, as your business evolves, you soon realize that spending time carrying out all these tasks, combined with the increasing stress caused by reactivity, prevents you from completing what's truly important.

There are two ways to approach this situation:

1. You can let yourself become totally overwhelmed, let stress build up, and eventually burn out.

2. You can see it as an opportunity to optimize how you manage your day-to-day operations.

Choosing option 2 means you'll have to start standardizing, which is a scary word for the passionate creative who is seeking freedom.

But don't be scared. Standardizing your repetitive and recurring tasks is the best thing you'll ever do to regain time freedom. The key lies in building structured processes. We call these processes "Routines." In the same way that we each need personal routines, your business needs routines of its own. I'll show you how to build them.

► How To Create A Standardized Routine

We're going to use the Routine Builder to bring structure to your recurring business activities. This tool will help you organize and document the tasks you do on a consistent basis, eliminating instinctive reactivity and freeing up space in your life so you can focus on what will move your business forward. Standardized Routines are the building blocks of a structure that ensures tasks are done properly, without chaos.

Here's how to create standardized business Routines:

Step 1: Identify Tasks & Group Them Together

Earlier, I asked you to take an inventory of your tasks and identify those you keep doing on a regular basis. These are your recurring tasks. Group them by theme, category, or purpose.

Let's look at an example. Suppose you use social media to grow your business. Perhaps you need to post on Instagram, Facebook, LinkedIn, YouTube, or other platforms every day or every week. Posting on each network is a separate task. Taken together, those tasks could make up a group, so they belong in the same category. Each group is the basis of a Routine.

Step 2: Name Each Routine

These names should be simple, descriptive, and memorable. Each name should sum up the nature or purpose of the tasks in the group. To avoid confusion, try not to have two or more Routines with similar names.

Step 3: Create A Clear Description

Write down why your Routine is important and how it will advance your business. This shouldn't require more than one or two sentences. If these answers don't come easily to you, you may need to go back to Step 1 and regroup your tasks, or perhaps eliminate some of them if they don't serve a clear purpose.

Step 4: Establish Frequency & Duration

Having identified your tasks and routines, you need to establish their duration and frequency. How often do you need to carry out your routines? Is it daily, weekly, or monthly?

In my case, as I'll show you shortly, I have a daily social media Routine. I go through a stack of tasks every day except weekends, and it takes me 30 minutes each time. But it might not be the same for you. The timing and frequency will depend on your personal situation.

Step 5: Outline Process Steps

Next, structure the process by outlining the steps you must take to perform your Routine.

To make it simple, here's a Routine Builder template you can use:

ROUTINE TITLE

DESCRIPTION

FREQUENCY

Daily   Weekly   Monthly   _____

DAY(S) OF THE WEEK

Mo.   Tu.   We.   Th.   Fr.   Sa.   Su.

DURATION

15 mins.   30 mins.   60 mins.   _____

PROCEDURE (STEPS)

1. _____

2. _____

3. _____

4. _____

5. _____

6. _____

7. _____

8. _____

9. _____

When you begin documenting your processes, you will soon realize that you've already been using routines in your business. However, to create space, you also need to recognize that you probably won't be able to keep doing everything yourself. This is where the next step comes in.

> Download the **Routine Builder** template at
www.DoneByNoonBook.com/Toolbox

► A Foundation To Properly D.O.A.: Delegate. Outsource. Automate.

I've got some bad news and some good news for you.

The bad news: You'll have to make difficult decisions. It's time to let go of some tasks that you are emotionally invested in.

The good news: By building your Routines, you're laying an excellent foundation that will empower you to achieve more leverage.

Earlier, I talked about the three Ss of leverage (Strengths, Structure, and Systems) to get powerful and sustainable leverage in your business. What you'll read next is an example of its practical application.

Standardization is the starting point of optimization. It makes delegating, outsourcing, and automating tasks a lot easier.

Before I show you examples of how to D.O.A. tasks, let's define these terms properly. Automating is self-explanatory; it simply means leveraging technology. Delegating refers to giving work tasks to internal employees, while Outsourcing involves hiring subcontractors from outside companies to perform the work. Delegating often means the person you will assign the task to will be on your payroll and usually work exclusively for you. When you outsource, it's usually either to an agency or a freelancer who has other clients.

Outsourcing is great for small businesses because it's a lot easier to control costs and doesn't require hiring someone full time when you don't need to. Subcontractors are also business owners who usually specialize in a specific field. Because they run their own businesses, they take their work seriously to ensure their clients are satisfied.

Quick Tip: Always treat a subcontractor as a member of the team. Even if a subcontractor only performs a few hours a week for you, always include them in your team communication channels.

This all sounds easy until you actually begin leading other people. Many entrepreneurs make the mistake of trying to offload everything they can't or don't want to do anymore onto one new hire. I call this "dumping." Dumping is when you simply assign work to someone without proper directions and guidance.

This is something I see many entrepreneurs who attempt to delegate or outsource do. They assume others will know what to do and exactly how to perform specific tasks. However, when things are not done to their standard, they'll blame it on the person they hired, saying, "It's easier to keep doing it myself because it's never done the way I want it."

The truth is you can't expect others to magically read your mind and "just know" how things should be done.

You'll miss the mark when delegating and outsourcing if you don't create a procedure for each task. To Delegate or Outsource properly, you need to be very clear on what you need and how you want it to be done, so there's no ambiguity or guesswork.

Consider how recipes work. A recipe is a standardized process for preparing food. It tells you exactly how much of each ingredient you need to use and how to combine them. As long as you follow the instructions, you'll get the same meal every time. If you give the recipe to someone else, they should get the same results.

By following a standard procedure, you'll know exactly what results to expect. If these processes aren't standardized, you're inviting chaos.

If you're just given the ingredients but don't get any instructions, it will be a lot more challenging to come up with the desired outcome, and your meal will probably not taste as good, even though you used the right ingredients.

That's why beyond building processes, creating a procedure is often key to properly D.O.A.

A procedure is a piece of step-by-step documentation that explains how something needs to be executed. It's one step deeper than the process. Think of a process as the outline of what needs to be done and a Procedure as the "How-to" for one or multiple steps of the Routine.

With that in mind, you'll need to identify the parts of a Routine that you don't want to perform and run it through the D.O.A. Map.

The D.O.A. Map is a simple tool that will help you decide if you need to Delegate, Outsource, or Automate a task. I'll show you how I use it specifically using two of my personal Routines in the next part.

Before you start optimizing, I need to give you a warning: You need to have a solid structure in place before you consider delegating, outsourcing, or automating. The problem is that most people try to take shortcuts without having a solid foundation. I saw this all the time in my career as a fitness coach. Most of my clients would take supplements in the hope of seeing fast and effortless results, only to suffer massive disappointment when they didn't have the desired effect. It's not that supplements don't work, but they are only effective in the context of proper training, nutrition, and basic fitness. When my clients came to see me, I took them back to the basics and helped them create a strong structure before optimizing. With this methodology, we're applying the same principle to your entrepreneurial life.

Another word of warning I'd like to share: Don't D.O.A. to increase your capacity. This is also a common mistake. Too many entrepreneurs think they can solve their problems by buying capacity without taking steps to increase space in their lives. But all too often, this actually creates more chaos.

D.O.A. to create space! When you have space in your life, you will automatically build capacity, but it doesn't always work the other way around. Using leverage to increase capacity does not always create more space. Don't focus on working more, but on working right.

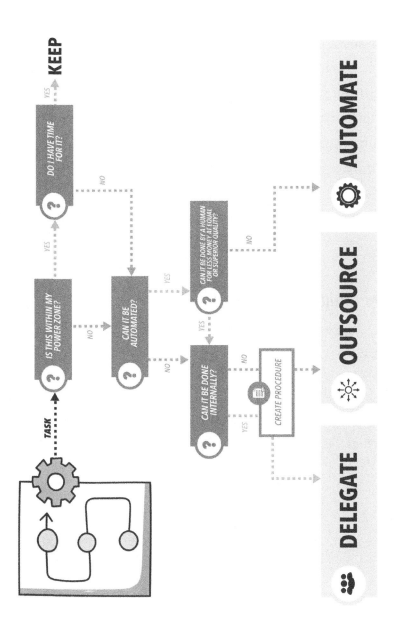

TASK

IS THIS WITHIN MY POWER ZONE?

YES → DO I HAVE TIME FOR IT?

YES → KEEP

NO → CAN IT BE AUTOMATED?

YES → CAN IT BE DONE BY A HUMAN FOR LESS MONEY AT EQUAL OR SUPERIOR QUALITY?

NO → AUTOMATE

YES → CAN IT BE DONE INTERNALLY?

NO → CREATE PROCEDURE

NO → OUTSOURCE

YES → DELEGATE

AUTOMATE

OUTSOURCE

DELEGATE

I'll get straight to the point: After the ability to lead yourself, your ability to D.O.A. will be the #1 factor for increasing your business growth and freedom.

If you want to harness the power of leverage, you need to structure all the recurring tasks that are essential to the proper functioning of your business by creating Routines, keep those aligned with your strengths, and gradually build robust systems to Delegate, Outsource and Automate the rest.

> Download the **D.O.A. Map** template at
> *www.DoneByNoonBook.com/Toolbox*

► Optimized Routine Examples

Here are two of my personal Routines that I will show you how to schedule in the upcoming chapter using the Done By Noon framework.

Routine Example #1: Social Media Activity Stack

Social Media Activity Stack

DESCRIPTION

My daily social media activity stack to ensure I have good presence and visibility on multiple platforms.

FREQUENCY

✓ Daily   Weekly   Monthly   _____

DAY(S) OF THE WEEK

✓ Mo. ✓ Tu. ✓ We. ✓ Th. ✓ Fr.   Sa.   Su.

DURATION

15 mins. ✓ 30 mins.   60 mins.   _____

PROCEDURE (STEPS)

1. Post on Instagram
2. Post on Facebook
3. Post on LinkedIn
4. Like 5 posts on each platform
5. Share 1 post/article on each platform
6. Reply to post comments on each platform
7. Reply to Private Messages on each platform
8.
9.

I follow a daily social media Routine, guided by a checklist. I interact on multiple platforms, including Instagram, Facebook, and LinkedIn, to raise awareness of my business and engage with people.

This is a 7-step process that is done every day. It now takes me 30 minutes daily, but it used to take up much more time. So, how did I get down to only 30 minutes?

First, the more times I completed the process, the better I got. Over time, as per the principle of adaptation, it required less and less brainpower, and I've become increasingly efficient. Second, I gradually optimized it using the D.O.A. Map. I could D.O.A. this Routine entirely but decided to still keep a few items that were directly linked to my personal strengths.

Here's how this Routine is optimized step by step:

Steps 1 to 4 are outsourced and automated

I used to create my posts myself. As the business grew, I had to look into outsourcing this part as it wasn't within my Power Zone. Now, I have hired a freelance content manager for a few hours a month to create these posts and schedule them.

She also takes care of the podcast distribution and social media content creation, turning podcast episodes into video cards, quote cards, and audio clips. She then adds the finished content in a database. We have premade templates that we use via cost-effective online software like Canva and Headliner. To eliminate reactivity, we make sure our podcast production is always scheduled eight weeks in advance.

In order for me to reclaim space, Steps 1 to 3 are taken care of by our content manager. She proactively plans a full month's content in advance before the month begins. From there, she schedules all the content to be posted automatically using a social media scheduler called SocialPilot. Once scheduled, pieces of content are automatically posted on Instagram, Facebook, and LinkedIn at the set date and time. No additional human action is required.

For Step 4, I also outsource the setup to our content manager and automate the posting. Our system is simple. When I see an article that I like, I bookmark it using a free browser extension called "Pocket" that saves the URL. My content manager has access to the now-massive database of articles that she can pick from and schedule one article to be shared daily using the same process as the other posts but to be delivered at a different time. This makes it easy for me to share useful, relevant content daily without having to produce it myself.

To ensure our social media manager knows exactly what to do, we created a procedure for her. Here's what the procedure my social media manager follows to create and schedule all the content for a month looks like.

How To Schedule Social Media Posts Using SocialPilot

- ☐ Plan a month's worth of posts using the podcast content database

  🔗 *Link to podcast content database*

- ☐ Using SocialPilot, schedule one piece of content related to that week's podcast to be posted each day at 8 A.M. on Instagram, Facebook, and LinkedIn. Follow this schedule:
  - ☐ Monday: Link to podcast episode
  - ☐ Tuesday: Audio card #1
  - ☐ Wednesday: Video card
  - ☐ Thursday: Quote card
  - ☐ Friday: Audio card #2

- ☐ Plan a month's worth of articles to be shared. Pick a daily article from the Pocket database.

  🔗 *Link to the pocket article database*

- ☐ Using SocialPilot, schedule each article to be shared at 3 P.M. each day on Facebook and LinkedIn.

Notes:

- ☐ Here is a link to the technical tutorial

  🔗 *Click here to view the SocialPilot scheduling video tutorial*

- ☐ Logins are shared via LastPass. If you don't have them, please contact Cedric at cedric@effic.co and ask him to share them with you.

This procedure is properly documented in a virtual binder which is called our Playbook. This database contains all the checklists we need to get things done in our company.

Take the example of Football (American Football for our European readers). A coach always has a playbook with a collection of plays that a team has practiced and could potentially run during a game. The offense, defense, and special teams will all have specific playbooks with the complete set of plays that can be called upon in each situation. To run a play, your players need to understand exactly how to run it. The playbook ensures it happens as planned.

Basically, a playbook lets you translate your vision and strategy into tactics. The playbook helps the team visualize what is needed to complete the play. A new addition to the team would need to have the plays explained to him before jumping on the field, especially if the play is very specific to the new team.

This is the same approach you need to have with your business. As an example, if something happens to my content manager, I can effortlessly outsource this procedure to someone else by giving them the process that's in our Playbook.

I keep Steps 5 to 7

As an extrovert and a people person, communication is a natural strength of mine. This strength is permanently in my Power Zone. That's why I usually like to keep all tasks that draw upon it.

Every day, I take a few minutes to browse my feed on each social media platform and "like" posts from my contacts that I find interesting. This allows me to have my name pop up regularly on other people's posts. When relevant, I also add a short comment.

I then reply to the comments on my posts. It's a perfect opportunity for me to engage with my community, build trust, and nurture relationships.

I also reply to my private messages daily. However, before replying to personal messages, I ask my assistant to take care of any customer service messages and to leave the rest to me. I generally use the audio message features to reply to my messages. It's not only efficient but it adds a personal touch that people like.

I also leverage my strengths for the next Routine below.

Routine Example #2: Top Clients Contact

ROUTINE TITLE

Top Clients Contact

DESCRIPTION

Reach out to my top clients of the previous week to create a personal connection with them and assist them if needed

FREQUENCY

Daily ✓ Weekly Monthly _____

DAY(S) OF THE WEEK

Mo. Tu. ✓ We. Th. Fr. Sa. Su.

DURATION

15 mins. ✓ 30 mins. 60 mins. _____

PROCEDURE (STEPS)

1. Pick 5 customers from last week's list

2. Record a Vidyard video for each of them

3. Send them an email each (with Vidyard link) · Use template

4. If they don't have my book, send it to them.

5. Support follow up 30 days post purchase

6.

7.

8.

9.

At Effic, we monitor returning clients using a spreadsheet that contains my top returning clients' details. Every Wednesday, I follow a 30-minute "Top Clients Contact" Routine. This process is a structured way of reaching out to them and is partly delegated.

I keep Steps 1 to 3

I pick the top five returning clients from a list that was automatically generated the previous week. I like to pick them up myself as sometimes, I see the name of a client I already have a connection with, and it's a perfect opportunity to reconnect. More than often, I will pick clients that are returning for the first time.

Next, I record a short video message for each of them. These video messages are quick to produce because I use a simple Chrome extension called Vidyard that records a video directly from my phone or computer and generates a link in seconds. The recipient simply needs to click on the link to view the video. In these video messages, I thank my loyal clients for their purchase. I tell them that I appreciate their business and build rapport to establish or maintain our connection by adding a personal touch to each of the videos. Sometimes I talk about something I know from their city, a local sports team, an event, etc. It just creates a better personal connection.

Then, I grab their email address from the spreadsheet, and send them this script below via my personal email:

Hi [first name],

Hope things are well in *[the city they live in]*.

I saw you placed a new order with us. Thanks again for being a loyal customer, it really means a lot to me and the team here at Effic that you love what we have created.

I also wanted to thank you in person, so I recorded this quick personal video for you this morning, check it out: *[link to video]*.

Have a great rest of your week.

Cheers,

Dave

PS: If you ever need anything, feel free to reach out to me directly

---

Note that I also add a personal touch to the email whenever possible.

With this simple process, I get to build meaningful connections with my clients. I get more referrals and get to meet our loyal fans. This process helps us connect with our clients on a deeper level and, by extension, grow our business. It takes only 30 minutes per week, and it has a huge impact.

Steps 4 and 5 are delegated

The rest of the tasks are delegated to my right-hand man, Cedric. Cedric checks our system to see whether the clients I contacted have a copy of my book. If they don't, he'll send them a copy as a gift, which is always well-received. Using our task management software, he sets up a reminder to follow up with clients 30 days later to see if they received their book and to ask if there's anything else we can do to help them. We currently use ClickUp as a task management platform. There are many other options available online, like Trello, Asana, Monday, Todoist, etc.

Note that there is also a procedure created for each task, safely stored in our Playbook, to ensure someone could take over when needed, especially when Cedric is on vacation.

These procedures are under the "Operations" part of the playbook and are named:

- How to send a book manually
- How to create a follow-up task in ClickUp

With one simple click, you'd know exactly how to do this as well.

As you can see, being proactive and documenting your key processes and subsequent procedures will ensure your repetitive and recurring tasks are optimized so that you can have more space and best leverage your strengths in order to reclaim your freedom.

That being said, Prioritization is only one piece of the puzzle. As Dr. Covey always said: *"The key is not to prioritize your schedule, but to schedule your priorities."* That's precisely what we'll show you how to do next.

Step Three

Planning

effic

At this point, we've established a clear guideline. We know where we want to go, and we have a set of clear directions that will take us there. Because we know where our priorities lie, we've successfully prioritized our tasks and know what we should be focusing on for maximum impact. Now I'm going to show you how to use our Done By Noon framework to plan and optimize your schedule for sustainable productivity.

A lot of people love the name: "Done By Noon." It's easy to see why. I mean, who wouldn't want to be done by noon? But here's the truth: You're not going to work for a few hours and then be finished for the day. This is not a planning system for lazy people. But for any entrepreneur who follows it properly, I guarantee it will be a game-changer.

The Done By Noon framework will make you think again about what a workweek could look like, and how you can build a schedule that is designed to help you work "right" rather than "more." You'll start to question conventional wisdom and instead discover what kind of schedule best suits your context.

Let's consider where our idea of the 40-hour workweek comes from. During the Industrial Revolution, it wasn't unusual for people to work 12 hours a day, 6 days a week. Then, in the 1920s, Henry Ford challenged that norm. He introduced a 5-day 40-hour workweek instead, while still paying his employees the same wages for fewer hours.

A 40-hour workweek may make sense for people who do physical labor for a living. However, does it make sense for entrepreneurs? If someone is using their brain rather than their body to create something, what's so special about 40 hours?

Here's something even more important to consider: How are those 40 hours being used? How much of that time is wasted? The way we work is starting to change, and it's pushing us to rethink what a typical work week should or could look like once again.

We are moving into a new period called the "Creativity Revolution." In the coming decades, robotics and automation will take over many jobs currently held by humans. But because robots will never be as creative as people (at least not for a very very long time), those of us who are creative and entrepreneurial will thrive.

"Doing" isn't the key to future success. "Creating" is. A time where creative entrepreneurs will shine more than ever.

Now, is it optimal for creative business leaders and big thinkers to work 40 hours a week? No. Should we keep applying a century-old concept that dates from the Industrial Revolution? Definitely not. As entrepreneurs, we need to set a schedule that allows for focused work optimally while protecting us against burnout. This is where the Planning step comes in, the most practical of the four steps.

FocusBoxing™
Time Blocking Optimization For
The Entrepreneurial Brain

We can't control time; at least, we can't control how much time we have, and we can't slow it down or speed it up. However, you can control what you do within the time you have available. This doesn't mean you need to schedule your life by the minute, but by organizing and optimizing your work time and proactively planning your tasks, you'll regain control over your business and life.

► Time Blocking Is Great But...

You've probably heard of time blocking. It's a simple time management technique that involves allocating a fixed, maximum unit of time for an activity in advance.

Time blocking is great to decide HOW you'll invest the external finite resource that is time. It's great when it comes to your personal life. However, when it comes to your workload, it doesn't free you from the burden of choice. If you're not proactive on WHAT you'll invest your two critical internal finite resources that are Energy and Attention, you will have to keep making moment-by-moment decisions about what you will do next because you won't have already made those choices. Falling back into a state of reactivity, the ultimate business enemy.

The key to making time blocking effective in a business context is to manage your focus within each block and optimize it over time.

► Focus = Energy + Attention

Focus can be defined as the intentional and proper investment of your energy and attention within a specific time frame. I prefer to think of these time blocks as boxes that need to be filled with specific content. That's why we call time block FocusBoxes.

Imagine you're standing in front of a large shelf. This shelf is your schedule. It's full of boxes, each representing a scheduled period of time. Every box contains a Focus that requires Energy and Attention. When you take a box down from the shelf and open it, you can only execute whatever task is stored within it. You can't have two or more boxes open at the same time. When the allotted time is up, you must close the box and place it back on the shelf.

Imagine if these boxes were empty when you opened them and you needed to fill them during the period of time allotted. You'd revert back to a state of reactivity, making trivial decisions about what you "feel" is important or urgent.

To avoid drifting, our work needs to be proactively Focus-Boxed. We need to be proactive and plan how we'll use our resources each day. You need to know in advance what you will be working on. Labeling time boxes is easy, but proactively planning what's in these boxes is what you'll learn to do correctly.

► The Cost Of Focus Shifting

An entrepreneurial brain is both a precious asset and an enemy. Like a mustang, it needs to be tamed. You can't trust your entrepreneurial brain when it comes to maintaining focus, and you need to create the best possible conditions to channel it properly.

In his bestselling book, Cal Newport explains his concept of Deep Work as *"the ability to focus without distraction on a cognitively demanding task."* When you schedule a chunk of time to work on a specific project, you'll need to bring all your mental resources to bear on that one thing. You can't spread your attention across multiple tasks. The better you become at singling out a task you want to accomplish, the easier it will be to put all your mental muscles to work and complete it.

You know what your priorities are and how to break down your tasks. Now you're going to have to fill your FocusBoxes accordingly, protect your focus, and combat the ultimate focus killer: focus shifting.

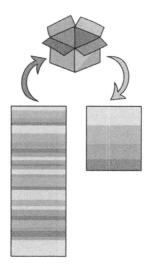

To stay on track, you need to avoid switching your focus back and forth between tasks. Many of us like to think that we're good multitaskers. As entrepreneurs, we often tell ourselves that we can focus on lots of things at the same time and do them all to a high standard. Unfortunately, multitasking research suggests otherwise.

In one study, a group of Stanford scientists set out to identify people who considered themselves to be gifted multitaskers and tested them to find out whether they really were better at switching between tasks compared with people who prefer to focus on one thing at a time.

The researchers recruited over 200 students to take part in a series of studies. First, they gave their participants a questionnaire asking them how many hours per week they spent multitasking. They used the results to classify participants into two groups: heavy and light multitaskers.

Next, they asked both groups to complete four tests that measured the participants' ability to switch between tasks. To the researchers' surprise, they found that the heavy multitaskers didn't outperform the light multitaskers. In fact, they performed worse on the tests. The supposedly "gifted" multitaskers struggled to filter out irrelevant information, organize their thoughts, and move between tasks.

Focus shifting also happens when we're interrupted. Interruptions can take different forms and might cost you more time than you realize.

Gloria Mark, a professor at the University of California, followed 24 employees at a tech firm for three days. By observing and interviewing her participants, Mark was able to learn how often the workers were interrupted, what kind of interruptions they faced, and how long it took them to resume their work.

She found that workers had to deal with two kinds of interruptions: internal and external. An internal interruption is anything that makes you decide to stop working of your own volition. For example, you might be in the middle of a task, start worrying about a meeting you have scheduled later in the day and lose your focus. External interruptions are caused by other people or your environment. For instance, a ringing phone is a frequent external interruption that triggers focus shifting.

In her research, Mark discovered that it takes over 25 minutes to refocus on a task after an interruption. If this happens to you several times per day, you could lose hours of time that could be spent on productive work.

When you focus on a single task, you can give it 100% of your attention. But when you start trying to switch between contexts, you start losing a lot of energy. Focus shifting carries a tremendous energetic cost. It forces your brain to adapt and refocus within a short period of time. For most people, focus shifting is a bad habit that requires discipline to break.

This doesn't come naturally to everyone, but with time, using FocusBoxing within the Done By Noon framework, you'll come to understand your modus operandi, how your entrepreneurial brain operates, and make the proper adjustments.

The Done By Noon® Framework

The Step By Step Plan To Create Your Done By Noon® Schedule

It's time to start using the Done By Noon framework.

When I started teaching this framework, it didn't have a name. I always began my sessions by asking my students this question: "If I told you that every single day, you had to be done by noon, how would you organize your schedule to grow your business without sacrificing what's important?"

Most of the time, the answer would be, "Oh… wouldn't it be nice to always be done by noon!" followed by laughter. Some students would then say, "It's like the 4-Hour Workweek... we all know it isn't possible." They always wanted to draw parallels between the two, and they didn't think either was feasible.

The concept of "Done By Noon" is appealing because it hints at freedom. However, we tend to take a narrow view of freedom and associate it solely with time. We think about how much time we'd like to have, and what we'd like to do with it. We think about spending time with family, spending time traveling, and spending time doing other fun activities.

People rarely think about creative freedom, even though a desire to create new things is what drives most entrepreneurs. Instead, we focus on time so much that we create a barrier between "business" and "life."

Just like the 4-Hour Workweek, the Done By Noon approach is not about doing less just for the sake of it. It's about building the right structure and systems so you can have the space to live your entrepreneurial life the way you want. It's a holistic approach that lets you harmonize all your work and non-work activities.

Using this framework, you can literally be done by noon— if that's what you really desire. Would this leave you feeling fulfilled as an entrepreneur? Probably not. Entrepreneurs love to work and create. Most don't want to stop their workday at lunchtime.

So now, I'm going to ask you the same question: If I told you that every single day, you had to be done by noon, how would you organize your schedule to grow your business without sacrificing what's important?

At this moment, everything that you've learned so far in this book should click.

The first steps involve properly scheduling your Focus-Boxes associated with the four types of entrepreneurial tasks. By planning them proactively and adequately, you will create space in your schedule that you'll apply to what's aligned with what you truly want.

It is also time to apply the Effic philosophy as you fill your FocusBoxes to improve your efficiency and achieve your desired outcomes. Over time, your goal should always be to optimize these FocusBoxes to reclaim more space.

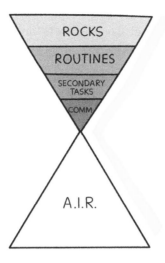

► Step 1: Schedule your Rocks

Every week, you'll need to proactively define your small rocks, your ProductivActions (or P.A. for short) that you'll work on. These are project-related tasks. I've already shown you how to break a big project down into small bite-size actions. Now we need to fit them into your schedule.

You've probably heard the expression, "Eat the frog first." This means that you should take the task you dislike the most and do it first. I don't like this concept. I think it's more helpful to think of the "frog" as the task that will take you the most energy, not the task you find most unpleasant.

Entrepreneurs love creating and working on new projects. However, we need to do that while still attending to everything else that's happening in our business. So, when I use the phrase "eat the frog" in the context of the Effic methodology, I'm referring to a high-impact task—a Rock—that carries a higher energetic cost.

Creativity is what drives growth and innovation in your business but also a big part of the entrepreneur's fulfillment, so Rocks need to be your first priority. They yield the highest return for your business in both the short and long-term, and must always come first. I'll show you an example later on of how this works in practice.

Step 1 Checklist:

- [ ] Schedule a 60 to 90-minute FocusBox every day to work on your Rocks. This FocusBox should be scheduled when you have the most energy available and are able to produce your most creative work.

- [ ] Proactively make a list of the small rocks you want to work on the next week by extracting small rocks (P.A.) from your Buckets.

- [ ] Allocate one small rock (P.A.) per FocusBox. You might be tempted to allocate more than one small rock, but it is recommended to focus on one small rock per FocusBox. More than often, you'll realize you can even break it down further, creating a series of smaller rocks to be even more focused. The goal is to build consistency when it comes to working on projects. Important projects are too often moved to the back burner because we simply "don't have enough time," this FocusBox ensures there is always time allocated to them.

► Step 2: Schedule your Routines

Now we're going to look at your other PowerMove: your Routines. These are operational tasks or processes that keep your business running. These will usually always be the same every week.

The goal is to contain them within a 30 to 60-minute Focus-Box, or a series of FocusBoxes. At first, you may need a little more time because they are essential to your business, but you cannot afford to spend your whole day working on Routines.

If you do, your life will start to resemble Groundhog Day, which is what business owners with high entrepreneurial drive fear the most. You must decide exactly when you start and stop working on your Routines. This forces you to stay within your Power Zone as much as possible and D.O.A. the rest. Once again, Routine optimization will be a key factor in reclaiming space in your schedule.

Routines always have a lower energetic cost, which is why it should come after the time you spend on your Rocks to mitigate stress that comes with effort. As you learned when we looked at the Impact Matrix, Routines have a high impact but a low energetic cost. Because you are comfortable performing these tasks, they don't require much effort or analysis. They come naturally, giving your brain the energetic break it needs after spending creative energy on your Rocks.

Step 2 Checklist:

☐ Schedule a FocusBox every day to work on a Routine. There can be more than one FocusBox, but I recommend trying to keep it within 60 minutes (example 2 x 30 minutes).

☐ Strategically place it at a time when you'd need an energetic break, usually after your Rocks FocusBox.

☐ Fill each FocusBox allotted to Routines by the items on your checklist for the Routine you want to perform that day.

☐ If you realize you have too many Routines, engage the D.O.A. Process starting with the ones further from your Power Zone.

► Step 3: Schedule your Secondary Tasks

The next step is to schedule your secondary tasks. These are your Reactive and Responsive Tasks, a direct result of your business activities and communications.

These tasks should ideally be the third part of your day because, as with Rocks, they have a higher energetic cost. If you begin your day with Rocks, then work at a lower intensity on your Routines, your mental batteries will then be recharged and ready for your secondary tasks. However, you won't need to push yourself hard for a long period; I recommend you work on these tasks for no longer than 30 to 45 minutes.

By scheduling these tasks and limiting the amount of time you can commit to them, you'll prevent the drift. This will eliminate firefighting and busywork that comes when you run a business based on urgency. Not everything is as urgent or important as you think it is. By limiting the number of secondary tasks you do and the time you spend on them, you'll become better at delegation, outsourcing, and automation. Again here, when you start with this framework, you might realize that this FocusBox isn't big enough. That's fine, but just like with your Routines, systematizing, optimizing, and delegating will be key.

Using FIONA's Desk will be a lifesaver, I can promise you.

Having a start and end time for your secondary tasks will limit reactivity and give you the space you need to create. Entrepreneurship is sparked by creativity, and it's vital to keep your creativity alive and avoid suffocating under a big pile of secondary tasks.

Step 3 Checklist:

☐ Schedule a 30-45 minute FocusBox every day to work on secondary tasks.

☐ Proactively make a list of the secondary tasks you intend to work on the next week by extracting them from FIONA's desk. You can use the Weekly List template you'll find in the Toolbox section on the website. Even though you want to plan to avoid urgency, it can and probably will still happen. You will have to add secondary tasks to your list as the week goes. If you realize you consistently have too many secondary tasks, even when using FIONA's desk, engage the D.O.A. Process.

☐ Allocate secondary tasks to each FocusBox. Limit the number of secondary tasks you proactively list. For example, if you use the Effic Planner, you'll notice you have space for only four tasks per day.

> Get the link to **FIONA's Desk** tutorial and download the **D.O.A. Process Map** and the **Weekly List Template** at *www.DoneByNoonBook.com/Toolbox*

► Step 4: Schedule your communication

Now it's time to schedule the time you spend on communication. The way you communicate will play a big part in the number of secondary tasks you'll have.

Communication plays a big part in business. We have to manage and respond to emails, instant messages, phone calls, and social media. We have to liaise with team members, talk to customers, and attend meetings. However, our ability to reach everybody quickly at any time of the day can become a major drift factor.

That's why I recommend that you allocate 30 to 60 minutes daily to communication. This includes emails, calls, messaging, and non-meeting team communication. By having a time cap, you will have to optimize the way you communicate. It will also limit the window of distraction opportunities.

Here's how to optimize your communications:

► If you use Social Media for your business, it should not be part of this time but should be made into a Routine just like I showed you earlier. You should also remove social media notifications and control access using a social media blocking app (I use the Freedom.to app) that will limit the amount of time you'll spend on it.

► Regular meetings like daily huddles or team meetings should also be considered Routines. These will force you to create frameworks to optimize them. Internally, we have condensed all our time sucking team meetings into a once a week 60-minute super meeting called the Momentum Meeting. It ensures we're always on the same page and that we make constant progress. You can consult the resources to download this framework.

► Direct talk time should be planned outside of daily communication. A FocusBox should be created to pro-actively insert meetings, long calls, lunches, interviews, etc. I'll show you how I schedule mine in an upcoming example.

► Reclaim control of your email inbox. Use the Inbox Freedom System available in the Toolbox. The Inbox Freedom System will walk you through regaining control of your inbox in just 15 minutes a day while systematically having an empty inbox each day. It will instantly cut the number of emails in your inbox by 70% or more without missing on important communications.

► Use a centralized communication hub platform and encourage asynchronous communication. We personally use an app named Twist (www.twist.com) to eliminate our team's need to spread discussions across email and chat apps by keeping information organized in one structured central place. FIONA's desk is located there, and even though it offers the possibility to chat live, we don't use this feature much. In fact, we avoid it unless it's a real emergency. That's why I hate Slack. It can be fun initially, but it rapidly becomes overwhelming. Projects get stuck in never-ending chats, information becomes nearly impossible to find, and always having the feeling like you're missing out increases stress and reactivity. The truth is work flows naturally when you're not pressured to respond immediately. Twist gives us the space to make progress on work that matters.

A lot of people don't do this. They don't schedule and optimize their communications or draw boundaries around the time they are and are not available to others. They make themselves available 24/7, which damages their productivity.

Step 4 Checklist:

- ☐ Schedule a 30-60 minute FocusBox every day for communications.

- ☐ Group all your communication together during that time (excluding meetings and social media)

- ☐ Optimize your communications.

> Download the **Momentum Meeting** template
and get the **Inbox Freedom System** at
www.DoneByNoonBook.com/Toolbox

► Step 5: Schedule your A.I.R.

I've forced you to imagine that you can only work by noon, so you prioritize your tasks accordingly.

A well-optimized Done By Noon schedule can help you achieve in 20 hours what you used to do in 40 because it pushes you to focus on your priorities. You've scheduled them properly because you have self-imposed limits on your time. In addition, the framework forces you to identify the nature of your tasks and limit the number you do each day in order to promote optimization.

By being disciplined and consistently looking at optimizing, you're going to see gradual results that compound over time. These results might not happen today or tomorrow, but if you dedicate time to mastering the methodology, it will become second nature. One or two years from now, you'll look back and be amazed at your progress. You'll find it hard to believe that you used to work so much without achieving your goals. Everything will be simpler; you'll be in control and achieve so much more in much less time.

This will have consequently freed up a lot of space in your schedule. The amount of new space available and how you'll use it will be contextual to your life and business with the unique factors that define it. We call them Focus Factors which include:

- The nature of your business.
- Your ambitions
- Your entrepreneurial drive
- Your team if you have one
- Your natural ability to D.O.A.
- Your family situation
- Your health
- Current events
- Any other individual and contextual factor can influence your life and business

That being said, better structure and systems will inevitably create space. This space is now open real estate for you to build on. And great news: you are in control. You can do whatever you want with it.

Really.

However, you'll have to make a choice. You can decide to go completely structureless in this new open space, which will ultimately lead you to revert to old habits and damage the structure you've built.

Or you fill this space with A.I.R.: Aligned Investments of Resources.

If there is one thing I want to get out of this book, it's this. The Done By Noon framework gives you space to do what is aligned with your broader vision. The term "investment" is important here because we are aiming for sustainability. I'm not talking about spending time, but investing it.

You need to do what yields greater dividends in the future.

You'll always get paid dividends when you manage your resources—time, energy, and attention—responsibly and adequately to get where you want to go.

If your goal is to create more, invest your resources towards it.

If your goal is to impact more clients, invest your resources towards it.

If your goal is to be with your family more, invest your resources towards it.

If your goal is to be healthier, invest your resources towards it.

If your goal is to build more wealth, invest your resources towards it.

Never compromise your alignment. This is your life, this is your business, and this is your freedom.

Truth is, most of us are primarily in business not just for one side of freedom but for all three sides—creativity, time, and money. Each side carries a different weight based on our individual alignment. It evolves with context, and we have to respect that.

When creating FocusBoxes, you've noticed that batching and theming are critical.

Task batching is when you group tasks together and schedule a block of time in which to get them done. Theming is when you group tasks of a similar nature together.

I invite you to do the same with your A.I.R. FocusBoxes. The key here is to do more of what fulfills you. For me, creating and building is what I value the most in my life and work. My A.I.R. needs to reflect it. I will show you exactly how I go about it in the next chapter.

Also, never schedule a FocusBox that is less than 2 hours to protect your focus. When you use larger FocusBoxes, you won't lose energy and attention focus shifting. Instead, because you'll only focus on one thing at a time, you'll enter a highly productive mental state that encourages creativity and productivity. This is called a flow state.

Psychologist Mihaly Csikszentmihalyi, an expert on the topic, defines flow in this way:

> *"...being completely involved in an activity for its own sake. The ego falls away—time flies. Every action, movement, and thought follows inevitably from the previous one, like playing jazz. Your whole being is involved, and you're using your skills to the utmost."*

Step 5 Checklist:

☐ Review alignment

☐ Decide how you'll invest your time, energy and attention within the new space available

☐ Create FocusBoxes of 2 hours minimum

☐ Use theming and batching

► Step 6: Schedule your personal activities

As entrepreneurs, we have no problems scheduling work. However, it's a different story when it comes to our personal lives. Business is a big part of who we are and takes up a lot of our time. It's a big part of our identity. But it's not all of it, and we need to build harmony between life and work. Being a dad/mom, a husband/wife, a religious practitioner, a crossfitter, a traveler, an advocate for a specific cause... These could all be parts of your identity alongside "business owner" or "entrepreneur."

Identifying yourself solely as an entrepreneur is dangerous. It's taking a narrow view of a more complex entity. We humans are one and multiple things at once. This is why I will always tell you that self-awareness and having a holistic view is key to your fulfillment not only as an entrepreneur but as a whole human.

Life and business go hand in hand, and they need to be integrated to be sustainable over the long term. So your family time, self-care, sports, and hobbies all need to be appropriately scheduled.

When you compare your personal and professional lives, you'll realize that both are made up of recurring tasks, especially if you have a family. Just like for your work Routines, standardize these tasks as much as possible. Implement a Routine for laundry, cooking, cleaning, and whatever recurring tasks you identify. Then, you can also go through the same D.O.A. process while keeping what you want to keep. Remember that it can take time as well. You might face obstacles in the form of resistance from your partner, financial limitations, or limited access to D.O.A. options. It's fine. Keep in mind that it's always a work in progress.

For example, I have a pretty sizable property where I live in eastern Canada, so I have a long driveway to plow in the winter and a large backyard to mow in the summer. I could spend many mornings and evenings a year plowing and mowing. I prefer to outsource these tasks. The money I'm investing there is a lot less valuable than the time I have with my family. Financially, it also makes a lot more sense. It costs me less to hire subcontractors than it does to buy and maintain my own equipment.

Don't feel guilty about not doing what you don't want to do. You shouldn't be guilted into living your life in a certain way. Instead, think about the space you'll gain where you can be present. Family breakfasts and dinners are a time to put my energy and attention on my family unit. These are non-negotiable and are always scheduled. I protect this time ferociously. No cellphone, no TV, no other distractions. The focus is on the family and nothing else. I invite you to do the same with your self-care, recovery, and deep thinking, which we'll cover later in the book.

Step 6 Checklist:

- ☐ Schedule your personal life Routines and activities.

- ☐ Standardize and optimize your Routines when possible.

- ☐ If you realize you have too many Routines, engage the D.O.A. Process.

► Step 7: Schedule Weekly Review

Step 7 is to schedule regular time for reviewing and scheduling at the end of each week. This time could be as little as 15 minutes, but it's essential. Personally, I recommend allocating 30 to 60 minutes. It's a powerful way to end your week, and this kind of reflection shouldn't be rushed.

In your Effic Planner, there's a page to help you do this every week. During this time, you'll evaluate what went well during the week and what adjustments, if any, you need to make. You'll then plan the next week.

No matter how successful and knowledgeable you are, there's always room for improvement. Regular reviews and adjustments create a continuous feedback system that will force you to develop your skills and move forward in your business.

Elon Musk, who is renowned for his productivity and many accomplishments, says, "I think it's imperative to have a feedback loop, where you are constantly thinking about what you've done and how you could be doing it better." He constantly pushes and questions himself, never content to stay still in business or life. Although he is extremely successful, he knows that there is room for improvement. You can always find a better way to do something. Regular reviews promote a growth mindset and constant improvement while still ensuring you remain true to your broader vision.

Here's what you need to do:

1. Review your annual guideline and quarterly buckets. Reviewing your annual guideline helps you keep in mind whatever it is that you want to see become a reality over the next 12 months.

   It's easy to get caught up in what's happening in your business. Even though you've set up your annual guideline and your buckets, you can still fall victim to the Drift. That's why you need to look at the guideline on a weekly basis. Review your quarterly buckets too. Go back to your list of small rocks and ask yourself, "What did I actually accomplish this week?" This will ensure you know where you're at with your projects.

2. List what you consider to be your three best small wins of the week. Often, as entrepreneurs, we only celebrate big wins. We tend to say, "Oh, this thing isn't big enough to celebrate." Don't do that. Acknowledge your victories as small wins that make you and your business better. They are important. If you have lots of wins, pick what you consider are the best three. There are so many things to celebrate in both life and business.

Don't neglect to acknowledge these things, as small as they can be.

3. Write down how you will celebrate your wins and progress. Personally, I love cigars and whiskey, so those are often my rewards when I want to celebrate a good week. I'm also an epicurean, as is my wife, and we regularly celebrate with a nice meal at one of our favorite restaurants. Whatever you enjoy, have a rewards system. Celebrating your small victories reminds you that you worked hard and that you deserve to reward yourself. You don't have to wait for someone else to tell you that you've done a good job.

4. List the obstacles you encountered during the week. What didn't go well? For example, maybe your kid got sick, and you had to go to the hospital, which put you behind. Or perhaps you spent too much time on social media because the memes were really funny this week. Look at the situation objectively and acknowledge the obstacles you faced.

5. Fill your basic self-awareness scorecard. This is a simple exercise to help you know yourself better. To fill the scorecard, rate between 0 and 5 how you perceived the following points in the past week:
   • Your overall energy level.
   • How clear and focused you felt mentally.
   • How productive you feel the week has been.

- How satisfied you are with your week overall.

Obviously, scoring five out of five on each measure would be ideal, but your scores will change based on your circumstances.

This exercise helps you understand your obstacles because if you get a low score on any of these measures, it suggests you've faced some challenges. Take a step back, gain some altitude, and ask yourself how you can make improvements next week. For example, if your energy levels are down, have you been getting enough sleep? You may need to plan an earlier bedtime. Personally, if I go to bed at midnight twice in one week, I'll be tired and miserable.

Remember, keep your broader vision and plan in mind as you strive for improvement. Whatever changes you make need to be aligned.

6. Go over your weekly notes. I always recommend taking notes and writing down ideas daily then organizing them by category (in the next part, I go through the IdeaBox, which will explain how I process ideas and notes). Some will become next week's tasks; others may simply act as a reminder. You might use your Planner for this, or keep a separate notebook. If your notes relate to a task, you can schedule it for next week.

7. Finally, make next week's list and refill your FocusBoxes.

Regular reviews promote growth and constant improvement while still ensuring you remain true to your broader vision.

Step 7 Checklist:

- ☐ Schedule a 15-60 minute FocusBox once a week, preferably the last FocusBox of your workweek.

- ☐ Go through the Weekly Review process

- ☐ Honor your commitment to Self-Leadership through respect, discipline, and awareness.

> Download the **Weekly Review** template at
> *www.DoneByNoonBook.com/Toolbox*

Doing this will require practice. It's a matter of breaking everything down, putting them in the right place, performing them at the right time, and tracking properly. When you keep doing this and gradually optimize, you'll see a compound effect.

The Done By Noon framework isn't a one-off tactic; it takes all the elements of the Effic Methodology combined together in a schedule. Structure creates freedom, and this structure creates sustainable freedom. It's worth the investment of time, energy, and attention.

► Don't Make These Done By Noon® Mistakes

Let's talk about the most common mistakes I see people make when using the Done By Noon framework.

Underestimating your workload and task completion times

You might find that a task takes much longer than you thought. We all do it. You'll likely make that mistake, especially when you first start working with a Done By Noon schedule. The key is to review and adjust. You can overfill a FocusBox, just like you can overfill a Bucket. You'll need to use your self-awareness, which will develop with time.

Research shows that we fall victim to a cognitive error called the "planning fallacy." Most of us make unrealistically optimistic predictions when estimating how long a task will take. Canadian researchers at the University of Waterloo published a study in *The Journal of Experimental Psychology* that explored this problem.

The participants in the study were psychology students in their final semester of an Honors Thesis course. At the beginning of the study, each participant was asked to estimate how long it would take them to finish their thesis. Later in the semester, the research followed the students' progress and recorded when they actually completed their projects. More than two-thirds of the students failed to finish their theses before their estimated completion dates.

But there's a twist to this story: The researchers had also asked the students to estimate when they would finish their projects if "everything went as well as it possibly could" and "if everything went as poorly as it possibly could." Almost half of them failed to finish by their "worst case" estimate.

These results show that when they try to plan ahead, most people assume that everything will go according to plan. They assume that the best-case scenario is the most likely, even though we all know from past experience that this is a dangerous assumption. If you make overly optimistic predictions, the amount of work you get done will fall short of your expectations.

Not being flexible

Scheduling doesn't mean overplanning. We can't be too rigid. The truth is that life happens. Business happens. Sometimes, a FocusBox will need to move somewhere else. You might need to close a box a little earlier than you expected. Sometimes you'll need to open it a bit later than you planned. That's fine.

One of my colleagues says that most very rigid productivity methodologies are always designed by 40-year-old single men with no kids. He's probably right. Many productivity methods are so rigid, the moment you apply a little resistance, it stops working.

Real life doesn't work like that. It can't be organized by the minute. This methodology is meant to be flexible. I want to hammer home the point that you're creating FocusBoxes and filling them with tasks and activities, and sometimes the contents of a box can change. Obviously, the rocks in your boxes will change over time as you work on a project. Routines can also evolve and be optimized. Rocks could be scheduled for the afternoon rather than the morning. You have to make it work within your own unique context.

You've also got to allow yourself time for unplanned things, even though you know exactly where it could fit into your schedule. For me, it's weekends where I have two full days of unplanned time.

Don't overplan. Overscheduling and overthinking are excessive, and an excessive approach never works in the long-term.

Forgetting context

A common mistake I keep witnessing is that entrepreneurs tend to go into "all or nothing mode." They will optimize everything so deeply that they forget the context.

The perfect example is when creating Routines in your personal life.

We can't escape things like laundry, cooking, and cleaning. These ensure the proper functioning of your household, just like the Routines you have in your business.

That being said, let's take the example of cooking. There can be two different contexts, each with a different intention.

One is to cook to feed yourself and your family—an everyday vital necessity. Having a set menu for the week with all the ingredients ready and the steps to prepare your meals will be a big factor in how much time you'll have to dedicate to the task.

The second one is cooking for the pleasure of it. For example, it could be cooking as a way to create a fun environment to be present with your significant other and deepen your relationship. Being present allows you to emotionally experience the moment for what it is without the mechanical "feeding as a vital necessity" part.

The bottom line: You need to build procedures to optimize cooking context #1 and regain space so that you invest more time in cooking context #2.

Schedule both. Standardize the mechanical, not the emotional. The intent of the Done By Noon framework is to have space to connect to your true self in your life and business, not turn you into a more productive robot!

Done By Noon®
Schedule Examples
How Personal Context And Mindset
Will Influence Your Schedule

I will now show you the many different forms a Done By Noon schedule can take.

The example on the next page is a classic Done By Noon schedule. It shows what your typical working week could look like.

For a very long time, my schedule looked very similar. However, the next schedule I'm going to show you is the one I use today. My schedule changed over time and in response to changing circumstances. For example, when my first daughter arrived, I had to modify it to accommodate my new context. When my second daughter was born, I had to change it again.

In other words, I had to move FocusBoxes around, and that's perfectly fine; when you use FocusBoxing, you create blocks that are easy to shift. It's like moving a box on a shelf. You know that each Box contains a unique focus. When you use a box, you can say to yourself, "This is what's in this box,

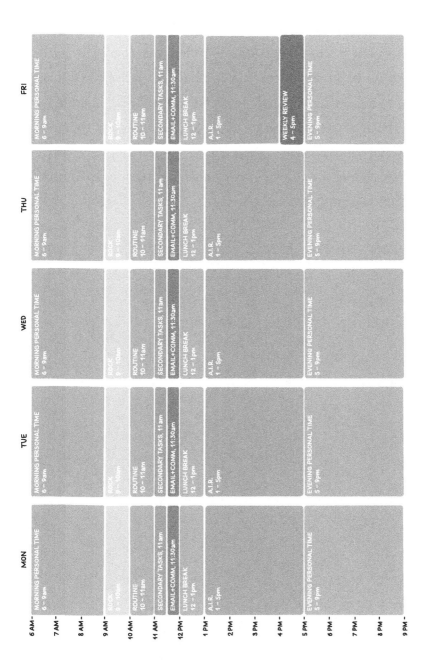

The weekly schedule grid shows the following time blocks:

MON
- MORNING PERSONAL TIME 6 – 9am
- ROCK 9 – 10am
- ROUTINE 10 – 11am
- SECONDARY TASKS, 11am
- EMAIL+COMM, 11:30am
- LUNCH BREAK 12 – 1pm
- A.I.R. 1 – 5pm
- EVENING PERSONAL TIME 5 – 9pm

TUE
- MORNING PERSONAL TIME 6 – 9am
- ROCK 9 – 10am
- ROUTINE 10 – 11am
- SECONDARY TASKS, 11am
- EMAIL+COMM, 11:30am
- LUNCH BREAK 12 – 1pm
- A.I.R. 1 – 5pm
- EVENING PERSONAL TIME 5 – 9pm

WED
- MORNING PERSONAL TIME 6 – 9am
- ROCK 9 – 10am
- ROUTINE 10 – 11am
- SECONDARY TASKS, 11am
- EMAIL+COMM, 11:30am
- LUNCH BREAK 12 – 1pm
- A.I.R. 1 – 5pm
- EVENING PERSONAL TIME 5 – 9pm

THU
- MORNING PERSONAL TIME 6 – 9am
- ROCK 9 – 10am
- ROUTINE 10 – 11am
- SECONDARY TASKS, 11am
- EMAIL+COMM, 11:30am
- LUNCH BREAK 12 – 1pm
- A.I.R. 1 – 5pm
- EVENING PERSONAL TIME 5 – 9pm

FRI
- MORNING PERSONAL TIME 6 – 9am
- ROCK 9 – 10am
- ROUTINE 10 – 11am
- SECONDARY TASKS, 11am
- EMAIL+COMM, 11:30am
- LUNCH BREAK 12 – 1pm
- A.I.R. 1 – 5pm
- WEEKLY REVIEW 4 – 5pm
- EVENING PERSONAL TIME 5 – 9pm

Time axis: 6 AM, 7 AM, 8 AM, 9 AM, 10 AM, 11 AM, 12 PM, 1 PM, 2 PM, 3 PM, 4 PM, 5 PM, 6 PM, 7 PM, 8 PM, 9 PM and this is what I have to focus on now." This doesn't mean the order of your boxes doesn't matter. They need to be optimized for the circumstances and consider your energy levels. But your boxes don't have to be fixed in one place forever. It's not necessary to have literally everything done by noon. If your business setup or personal life doesn't allow you to set up a schedule that ensures you get literally everything done by noon, that's fine. The key takeaway is that I schedule each FocusBox at the appropriate time.

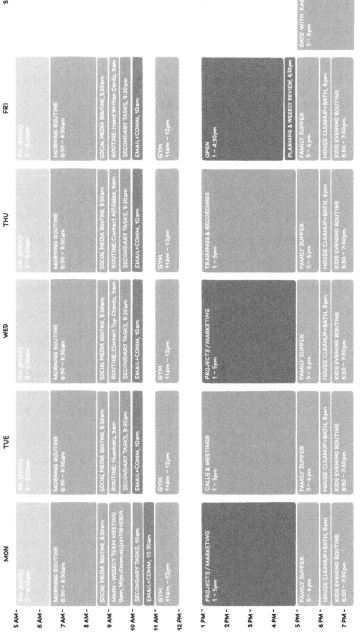

Dave's Entrepreneurial Done By Noon Schedule Example

Personally, I'm a classic "Done By Noon" practitioner, meaning that I prefer having all my baseline workload taken care of before noon. To create my schedule, I use Google Calendar and color-code each type of FocusBox. Feel free to use whatever scheduling app and calendar you want. I like Google calendar for its easy integration with many automation tools, but again this is just my personal preference.

1. **FocusBox #1: Rocks** - I schedule my priority action, a Small Rock, from 5:00 AM until 6:30 AM. I start every day by working on my Rocks for 90 minutes. Specifically, I work on one of the small Rocks that I've identified and listed in my planner. Setting up my schedule this way means that the first thing I do in the morning is work on my Rock that will bring a project forward. It ensures that I stay consistent in working towards a goal that's going to give me meaningful results. I know you're thinking, "Oh OK, you're done by noon because you wake up at 5:00 AM. But that wouldn't work for me." Think again! You don't have to get up at the same time as me or follow my schedule exactly. This is just how I schedule my morning routine so I can be there for my kids and get some gym time before lunch.

Now that my kids have regular sleeping patterns, I prefer working on my Rocks first. It's predictable. They usually wake up between 6:30 a.m. and 7:00 a.m., and my main priority is to be there for them. However, before I had this level of stability, the morning routine was the first item on my schedule, and it was a larger Box so I could fit in a quick workout as well. The kids dictated our wake up time, and it was highly unpredictable. My first-born was not a sleeper, and we never knew when she'd wake up. I had placed my 90-minute Rocks FocusBox after the morning routine, from 8:30 a.m. until 10:00 a.m. Honestly, I never was a morning person, but when I started the practice of waking up early before the children consistently, I created better quality work. It took me a few weeks to adapt, but it was a great upgrade for me personally. I truly enjoy this magic quiet time. I invite you to try it as well.

2. **Personal Time: Morning Routine** - Between 6:30 a.m. and 8:30 a.m. is my morning routine. I take care of my family, cook breakfast for my daughters, spend time with my wife, and most of the time, I have time for myself too, where I perform some items on my self-care routine. Self-care is crucial. You'll learn more about the basic daily self-care items in the next phase of the Effic methodology.

3. **FocusBoxes #2 and #3: Routines** - By 8:30 a.m., my kids are usually at school, and I'm ready to resume my work. Next on my schedule are Routines. You might have one or multiple Routines. Personally, I have 2 Routine Focus-Boxes that take 60 to 90 minutes in total. Here is how I fill these FocusBoxes weekly:

- Every single day, I go through the social media process I outlined in the Routines chapter. Over time, I highly optimized this Routine by delegating, outsourcing, and automating all the content posting so that I don't have to spend much time on social media. Because the time is limited, I don't open the door to any distractions. I've disciplined myself over time to treat social media as a business tool and not an entertainment medium. Everything I do on social media is intentional and scheduled. I made it a Routine because it's an essential part of the business in terms of operations and continuous growth.

- My second Monday Routine is a weekly team meeting. We use a framework called the Momentum Meeting that allows us to condense a week's worth of meetings down into just 60 minutes. You can check it out in the resources section. You might ask, "Dave, isn't that communication?" You're right. It is. However, by optimizing the process, I made it into a Routine. This means we don't have multiple unstructured, reactive meetings scattered throughout the week. However, by optimizing that weekly meeting with my team and making it a Routine, I gained a lot of productivity over time.

- On Tuesdays, I look at numbers for 30 minutes. I look at the previous week's KPIs like gross sales, traffic, conversion rates, R.O.A.S., A.C.V., and many others. Those numbers tell me what I can improve and create new marketing pieces accordingly. It's essential that I stay on top of these figures.

A lot of my Routines revolve around connecting and building relationships. Connecting with people and building great relationships is one of my superpowers, my Power Zone revolves a lot around my communication abilities. I love connecting with others, and it is always a strength that serves my business tremendously. It's something that has always worked extremely well for me, and it comes naturally. It doesn't take me a lot of energy to reach out to people, talk to them, and build great relationships that bring my business forward.

- On Wednesdays, I reach out to some of our top clients from the previous week using the process outlined in details in the Routines chapter.

- On Thursdays, I contact our affiliates. A lot of our business is done through our many affiliate programs that offer awesome commissions in exchange for referrals. So, during this time, I connect with my affiliates to see if I can help them sell our products and grow their businesses.

- On Friday, I have a routine that may seem a little strange and old school. I write handwritten cards and send them to business partners, colleagues, friends, and anyone else who has impacted me and my business in some way. Something I do regularly is sending a handwritten card to someone I look up to, that I don't know but would like to get to know. I write messages like, *"Thank you so much for what you do. You've inspired me, and I hope we cross paths one day."* You'd be amazed by the number of people who reply. I don't ask them for anything. These cards are just simple thank-you notes. I aim to write three cards each Friday. It's a straightforward 30-minute routine, but over time I've realized that building relationships gives the greatest return in my business. It's something I can do for a long time to come, if not forever, and it will keep yielding sustainable results.

You see, your Routines could be just 60 minutes of specific tasks every week, or they could be the same set of tasks every day. It depends on the kind of business you have and how you operate it.

4. **FocusBox #4: Secondary Tasks** - Next in my schedule is a 30-minute FocusBox for secondary tasks. Obviously, I limit the number of secondary tasks that I do daily. When it comes to reactivity, not everything is urgent or important. Some are; things come up that need immediate attention. However, I prefer to use a more proactive approach when it comes to tackling reactive tasks, so I schedule time every day to deal with them.

5. **FocusBox #5: Emails & Communications** - After my secondary tasks, I move onto emails and communications. This FocusBox has been extremely optimized over time using the tools and techniques I outlined in step 4.

6. **Personal Time: Gym** - Next is one of the key items in my self-care: exercise. I exercise daily for about an hour. Sometimes less, rarely more, but it's a non-negotiable event daily. I also find that placing exercise as a bridge between morning and afternoon increases my energy levels. My will power, my creative output, and my mental clarity is always improved.

7. This is followed by a 60-minute open window. I use this window mostly for my post-workout shake, shower, or to perform daily self-care items I couldn't perform in the morning. Sometimes I use it for lunch with Karine. Other times it will be used to make up for an emergency I had to deal with (let's say my secondary tasks took a bit longer that day and could only get to the gym half an hour later than my scheduled time). I prefer to keep this time completely open to allow flexibility.

8. **FocusBox #6: A.I.R.** - In the afternoon, I theme my Aligned Investment of Resources (A.I.R.). Because I've prioritized my tasks and optimized my schedule in a way that creates sustainability, I can theme this time to achieve better, faster results. You can see how I've broken it down in my schedule. Obviously, you don't have to theme your

A.I.R. in exactly the same way. You need to make it fit your business.

I give a theme to the rest of the day. I know that this box of time is there and that it's my focus for the rest of the day. I don't work on a multitude of different things at once. It also gives me a lot more flexibility.

The Done By Noon schedule ensures you never miss anything through consistency and momentum; you can then more easily adjust how you invest the rest of your energy and attention.

Sometimes, I will need to put out fires. Urgent, unexpected tasks come up. I'm not immune to them even though I structure everything to prevent them. If that happens, I want to make sure I can restructure what's in my A.I.R. FocusBoxes. I may decide to sacrifice a "Projects & Marketing" FocusBox that week because I had to deal with an unforeseen problem. That's fine. I know I'm never behind since my workload is always under control. It will just temporarily reduce my speed. That's because I use two FocusBoxes weekly to create.

Building products is also within my Power Zone, and properly aligning the investment of my resources in this individual ability allows me to finish a product faster or adjust my marketing campaigns quicker. Speed is one of the most important life and business assets you can have. Whatever context you're in. But, because I value my personal life as much as my professional life, it also offers me a lot of flexibility.

For example, when I travel to speak at a conference, I don't like working on projects. I prefer using this time to network and discover the city. I plan to make sure I'm always ahead on the project before I leave, never behind. I want to make sure to avoid "being late on project stress."

Other times, if for a specific week, my Tuesday and Thursday afternoons aren't busy, I group them in one afternoon and take the other afternoon off. I'll look at the weather and choose the most beautiful afternoon. Often I'll go to the beach with the family, go on a date with my wife or go fly fishing, for example, depending on the context that week.

Here's how I go about my A.I.R. FocusBoxes:

- On Monday, the theme of my A.I.R. is projects and marketing. It's a four-hour time slot. Sometimes I'll take three hours, sometimes two. It depends on my energy level and the nature of what I work on.

- On Tuesdays, I batch calls and meetings. I make a lot of calls: sales calls, follow-up calls related to specific projects, or calls with one of my teams. Because I batch my calls, everyone knows that Tuesday afternoon is when they're going to happen.

- On Wednesday, I have another FocusBox for projects and marketing. If you have a marketing department, that could be a good time for you to work with your marketing team. Or, if you do marketing yourself, you need to schedule a time for that. Sales and marketing will bring great results to your business. You can have marketing projects that are part of a Bucket, but you'll probably have ongoing marketing tasks, such as ad campaigns, that you'll need to work on regularly. Whatever you do in this time, it needs to be aligned with your vision but also with what you do well.

I want to emphasize that I'm in control of my workload. If I want to have more free time one quarter, I can simply leave one of my Buckets empty for that period. This means my workload will be lighter, and I can direct my A.I.R. toward something else, such as personal projects or traveling. Another way to reduce your workload is to Delegate, Outsource, or Automate more of your tasks.

- Thursdays are for training and recordings. For example, I might record training videos for my Effic Certified partners and coaches. I can also use this time to record podcast episodes or take the time to be a podcast guest. If I need to make a video, I do that on a Thursday. The fantastic thing about theming is that it gives you a specific context and framework for each time block. This means you don't have to switch back and forth between multiple contexts and mindsets.

- I keep Friday afternoons open. Keeping one box accessible means you can move others around if an emergency comes up. For example, let's say you have an emergency on Monday and need to move your projects and marketing box. If you keep Friday open, you can move it there instead. What I do on Friday will depend on what happens each week. More than often, I will use it as a time to do some deep thinking in order to make better decisions. Deep thinking allows me to always see the Big Picture with absolute clarity and keeps my ability to break down the vision into actionable steps very sharp. In the summer, I also love to take that time off to go on impromptu afternoon dates with my wife, go fishing, do some gardening, or simply enjoy my property.

- No matter what happens, my last FocusBox of my work week is my 30-minute weekly review and next week's planning. It ensures I have time to review my past week properly, and I know exactly what's coming up the week after. When I show up for work on Monday, I know how it will pan out. You might need more than 30 minutes; it could be an hour. It depends on you. I've been doing this for a long time, and planning is now second nature for me because I know how to work the methodology, but you might need 90 minutes on Friday for planning and reviewing your work. That's okay. If I decide to take Friday afternoon off, I move the planning box so it's immediately after email and communications, and I'm done for the day.

9. **Personal Time: Evening Routines** - No matter what happens, I have a strict 5:00 p.m. cut-off time. My personal, recurring non-work time is always scheduled. After I perform my "Checkout" ritual, it's 100% family time. It's non-negotiable in the Ruel household. We do this because when the kids came along, Karine and I found that it's very easy to just keep working through the afternoon and evening. The next thing you know, you have to tell the kids, "Dad has to work late today, so he's not eating with us. He's in his office." That's not what I want to do. Family is extremely important to me. It's a top priority. In the next phase, I'm going to show you how to do an evening checkout that helps me trigger the transition from work to family time.

Your situation might be different, but in my case, this time needs to be scheduled. Karine also has various Routines in place for the management of our family life. I'm giving some very specific and personal examples here; perhaps you can relate to them on some level. Either way, you need to make a schedule that works for you.

10. **Personal Time: Date with Karine** - Shortly after my first daughter was born, I decided to stop working during weekends. Now my weekends are always open. I don't like to schedule anything during that time. Sometimes, I'll have

a Routine popping up like the annual "Christmas House Decorations" one or the quarterly "Filter Replacement & Cleanup" for our air and water systems. However, there is one thing that never changes: the weekly date with my wife. By dating each other weekly, our marriage is strengthened. It's a non-negotiable time just for us. It allows us to focus on our connection completely. If you're married, it's a Routine I strongly recommend you implement, if you haven't already.

As you can see, my schedule is pretty full. But here's the key: Everything that needs to be accomplished and is essential for the proper functioning and growth of my business and life is taken care of. The example I've given you is my version of a Done By Noon schedule, but I hope it will provide you with a clear idea of how you can adapt it to your context. Change the times and boxes to make it work for you.

Founder Mindset vs. Owner-Operator Mindset

Now you might be asking, *"Dave, I have a service business. It requires me to work one-on-one with clients. Will this work for me?"*

Maybe you're a massage therapist, a personal trainer, an insurance broker, or any other kind of service provider. The answer is, "Yes, absolutely." However, you'll have to use the methodology differently based on your mindset.

As explained in Step 5, the way you will schedule your A.I.R. will be influenced by multiple focus factors. Besides uncontrollable life events related to health, family, or other world events, the defining focus factors will always be your ambitions, your entrepreneurial drive, and your natural ability to lead. The focus factors are a direct representation of your entrepreneurial mindset.

There are two typical types of entrepreneurial mindset: the Founder mindset, and the Owner-Operator mindset.

To illustrate this, let's use the example of two physiotherapists: Charlene and Greg. They each operate their own clinics. You'll see how these two professionals in the same field have entirely different schedules.

They both started with similar, full schedules with lots of focus shifting in their business. However, Charlene clearly has a Founder mindset, while Greg's style reflects an Owner-Operator mindset.

Let's see how we adapted their schedules to suit their individual styles using the Done By Noon framework.

Greg's Schedule (Owner-Operator Mindset)

Greg is a 42-year-old man. He's married and has no kids. He has been operating his practice for 11 years now. Greg is known to be very versatile and successfully tackles multiple client problems within his practice. Most of his clients come to him with back and hip pain, but he treats all kinds of injuries. He loves to do an in-depth analysis of each patient's individual problems.

Here's how Greg organizes his schedule based on the Done By Noon Framework:

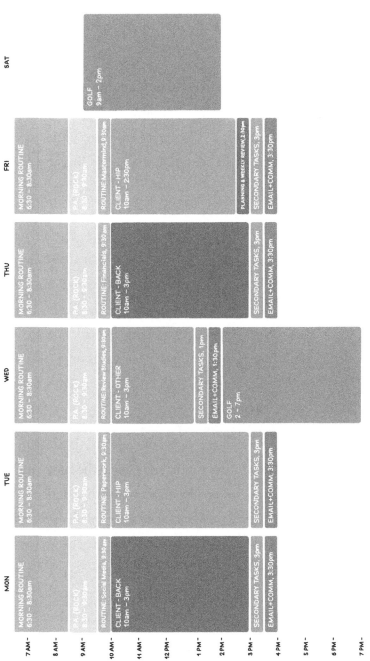

Greg's Done By Noon Schedule (Owner-Operator Mindset)

- Each day begins with a 2-hour window for daily self-care. He performs the same one you'll see later in the Protection phase.

- His first work-related FocusBox is for working on his projects. In Greg's case, projects take up less space as his main goal is not to create but to serve. However, Greg cares about operating a business that can adapt to new contexts and remains relevant. He likes to innovate and improve his current business structure. That's why he has what we call a "Maintenance Bucket" each quarter. He uses this Bucket to maintain an up-to-date practice (branding, marketing, client experience, etc.). I highly recommend most entrepreneurs have this type of Bucket on their quarterly buckets load. I personally always carry one. Creating new things is important, but maintaining and updating what you currently have is equally essential.

- Next up is a Routine. Greg only has one daily Routine, and it revolves around catching up on the latest studies in his field, staying on top of his paperwork, and keeping his social media updated. His social media posting is optimized and only needs one Routine FocusBox a week to schedule his weekly posts in advance. His last Routine on Friday involves catching up with a mastermind group of fellow physiotherapists who share their successes and challenges on a weekly basis. It keeps Greg accountable, and it helps him to know that every week, he can talk to a group that understands his business context.

- To combat focus shifting and make the best use of his energy, Greg batches the three different types of clients he serves based on their problems:

    ° Mondays and Thursdays are for clients with back problems
    ° Tuesdays and Fridays are for clients with hip problems
    ° Wednesdays are for clients with any other type of injury

This allows him to stay in context most days. He doesn't have to completely change his equipment and set-up between each patient. What changes with each client is the little particularities each patient has, and this is what Greg loves to tackle. He loves working attentively and being precise. When you think about it, his work consists of a series of processes that are standardized in Greg's head. He knows how to fix these problems, and he has procedures that he has developed over his many years of experience. However, Greg does not document these processes explicitly as he intends to remain a one-person operation.

To use another example, this approach could also work well if you were a fitness trainer. You could batch your clients who want to build muscle on one day and batch your clients who wish to reduce their body fat and tone-up on another. This way, you won't have to keep switching contexts. Try to set ground rules and lay down some boundaries. Sometimes we are too accommodating when setting our schedules. Instead, tell your clients the times you have available first and ask them what time they prefer within this time frame.

- Greg loves to golf in the summer. He wants to play golf twice a week and arranges his schedule accordingly, so it remains flexible. It's hard to predict with absolute certainty when he will play because the sport of golf is weather dependent. Greg usually evaluates the weather forecast a week to 10 days prior. Most of the time, he doesn't have to make any changes as the weather is mostly nice where he lives. However, sometimes he does.

In Greg's schedule above, you'll see Golf scheduled on Wednesday. This Box can be moved to the most favorable day of the week. To make this work, he never overfills his daily client FocusBoxes. For example, if he sees that the weather is great on a Thursday, he can ask a client to come in on Wednesday instead to open up time on Thursday. This flexibility means he can get on the golf course for a 2:30 p.m. tee time. This used to be less than ideal as Greg always had to make a few phone calls to reschedule a few people, but Greg has now hired a Virtual Assistant, Beth, who works for him a few hours a week and takes care of the rescheduling for him. She also takes care of invoicing customers, bookkeeping, ordering supplies, booking golf tee times, etc.

Greg also has a Saturday morning block of time dedicated to golfing. When the weather forecast is favorable, he will keep it there. If he sees that one of the upcoming weekdays will have great weather and that Saturday's forecast isn't so good, he'll decide which Client Focus-Box can be moved to Saturday. He also loves it when it's unchanged because his wife can come play with him. She enjoys golfing as well, but as an employee, she doesn't have the same flexibility, and weekends are her only option.

- Each day, Greg ends with a 30-minute FocusBox for secondary tasks and another one for communications. Greg has an online booking app, which saves him a lot of communication time, but he still has a few clients who call for information.

If you have a more reactive business, schedule secondary tasks and communications at the end of the day. If you do it earlier, it will create stress and anxiety because you'll be thinking about these tasks while you're working with your clients. You'll lose focus. Once you've finished your client work, you can do your secondary tasks and then finish the day with your emails and communications. The key is to understand that if you have any flexibility when it comes to your schedule, you have a responsibility to organize and optimize it based on your circumstances.

Charlene's Schedule (Founder Mindset)

Charlene is a 29-year-old woman. She is in a domestic partnership and has a six-year-old son named Jake. She has been operating her practice for three years. Charlene is a knee pain specialist, especially when it comes to post-ACL surgery rehabilitation. She has developed a very effective protocol for it, which has yielded great results for her clients. From the beginning, it was clear she never wanted to do client work for the rest of her life. She wanted to open more clinics. She saw herself be the CEO but not be caught in the day to day execution of treatments. She's very confident in her protocol. It's unique, and she wants to impact more clients with it. She also has a six-year-old son named Jack, and she wants to have time with him too."

It's evident that she had a Founder mindset, and she needed to structure her life and business to match her ambitions, drive, and family goals.

Here's what she did first:

- She trademarked her protocol and created a clear, documented, step-by-step process to treat patients using various standardized procedures that take them from point of diagnosis to full recovery. That allowed her to safely delegate her intellectual property, create a stronger brand, and open up the possibility of franchising her business.

- She hired another physiotherapist, Sarah, to reclaim space in her schedule. Sarah will take care of patients from 9 to 5 every weekday. Charlene will use this space to work on expanding her business. Her employee will use her well-documented protocol to treat patients.

After doing that, here's how Charlene organized her schedule based on the Done By Noon Framework:

- Each day begins with a 3-hour "Morning Routine" window for Charlene's self-care routine and having time to be with Jake and her partner.

- She begins each workday with her Rocks. To make her second clinic project a reality, she has filled three Buckets:

    ° **Bucket 1: Business Standardization,** which contains everything she needs to "copy and paste" standardized procedures and practices over to her new clinic.

    ° **Bucket 2: New Branding,** which contains everything she needs to improve her clinic's brand, thereby making it easier to duplicate and possibly franchise her business in the future.

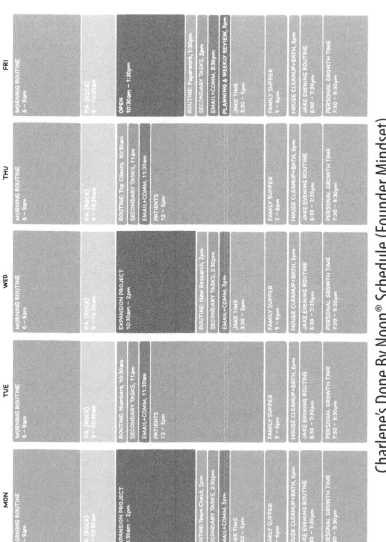

Charlene's Done By Noon® Schedule (Founder Mindset)

- ° **Bucket 3: Second Clinic Logistics,** which contains all the steps Charlene needs to take when obtaining and furnishing another space. It also includes tasks relating to finances, insurance, legal matters, etc.

- Three A.I.R. FocusBoxes are scheduled in the newly available space. Two are labeled "Expansion Project." These will be filled with tasks that will ultimately allow Charlene to open a second clinic. The third is labeled "Open" to give her flexibility. However, she has decided that most of the time, this FocusBox will be relabeled "Expansion Project." On Monday, Wednesday, and Friday, Charlene has scheduled them directly after her Rocks so they can act as an extension of that FocusBox. This way, she ensures she can get into a state of flow when needed.

- On Monday and Tuesday afternoons, Charlene keeps two time blocks open for work with athletes (her favorite group of clients).

- She has grouped her three other Done By Noon Focus-Boxes (Routines, Secondary Tasks (Reactive) and Communication (Responsive) together. Each FocusBox is a 30-minute time slot.

  - ° On Monday, Wednesday, and Friday, the group is scheduled after the A.I.R. FocusBox so she can stay in a state of flow with no interruptions to her project work.

- On Tuesday and Thursday, Charlene has scheduled them after her Rock FocusBox in order to completely focus on her patients for the rest of the day.

- Charlene fiercely protects her family time. When she was setting up her schedule, she decided that she wanted to be home by 3:30 P.M. as often as possible. Being back this early allows her to welcome Jake home when he gets off the school bus and have time with him. She has designed her schedule accordingly so she can do that on Monday, Wednesday, and Friday. It's a precious time for just Charlene and her son. Her partner welcomes Jake home every Tuesday and Thursday. Weekends are always free from work and focused on family activities. It's a non-negotiable for Charlene.

- Charlene's weekday evenings are very similar to mine. I think most parents will recognize this pattern. For Charlene, scheduling her family time from 5:00 P.M. until Jake goes to bed works perfectly.

- She also sets aside personal growth time in the evening. These action steps made Charlene understand that if she wants to grow, she needs to stop "doing" and start leading. She is learning how to do this by reading and taking online courses about team building and leadership.

In these two examples, everything has been accomplished by the end of the day. All tasks are accounted for. It's important to understand that it's a flexible environment; Greg and Charlene adjusted it to suit their own lives, business styles, and mindsets.

Own It!

We are all business owners, but we don't all have the same mindset. Entrepreneurs with an Owner-Operator mindset will operate their business more like a job. They write their own paychecks, but they want to keep "doing" the work. There is absolutely nothing wrong with that. Just like Greg, who knows that he loves working one-on-one with different types of clients, you need to have self-awareness to understand what fulfills you.

Greg now owns his ambitions, drive, and style. However, this wasn't always the case. At first, Greg wanted to expand his business and wasn't operating his practice like he is now. Initially, he was confused about why he was resisting change. The only way to get the answer was to take a deep look inside himself. Greg realized he felt pressure to grow based on what he sees others doing (ambition appropriation). He never wanted to build a team. Greg loved client work and wanted to keep doing it. It fulfilled him completely. For him, his creative freedom came in understanding a patient's problem and fixing it based on their individual needs. His business was already giving him the financial freedom he wanted. He understood the need to be true to himself, own his ambitions, and take the steps needed to move towards his vision while staying aligned.

Charlene, on the other end, had a higher entrepreneurial drive. Her creative freedom, like most entrepreneurs with a Founder mindset, lies in the opportunity to keep building. Just like Greg, she had already built a good level of financial freedom through her business. However, she craved more impact, which is often the case with entrepreneurs with Founder mindsets who haven't been infected by greed. She wants not only to impact more clients but also to impact the community of women entrepreneurs. She's also very fulfilled by her role as a mother to Jake, and she wasn't willing to sacrifice this role while growing her business. She scheduled her life and business accordingly, and it works well for her. Charlene owns her ambitions, drive, and style.

Remember what I said about working RIGHT? This is what it looks like. It's not that one approach is better than the other. The important thing to note is that in both cases, these business owners have aligned their approach with their big picture.

Step Four

Protection

effic

Let's move onto the fourth step of the Effic methodology. It's unique; other systems simply don't include it. We call it "Protection."

The goal of this phase is to protect your three finite resources: time, attention, and energy. Protection is made up of routines, habits, and rituals that will help you place guardrails around what you worked so hard to build in the first three phases.

What you'll learn in this phase will keep you on the road as you move along your journey to achieving your big goals. You will protect your time by safeguarding your structure. You will protect your attention by safeguarding your focus. Most importantly, you will protect your energy by safeguarding your physical, mental, and emotional health.

Protection is a critical part of the Effic methodology because it solidifies what you've done and created so far. Without it, you'll easily fall back into old ways of working and do things the way you've always done them. You'll find yourself saying things like, "Oh, that didn't work," not realizing that the real problem is that you haven't protected what you've already built.

This step also protects you from burnout. Burnout is caused by physical, mental, and emotional exhaustion. If you don't protect yourself, it doesn't matter how performant you are—there's a high chance you'll burn out. Protection keeps you performing at a sustainable level.

These habits, routines, and rituals have been a game-changer, not only for me but for the thousands of people who have gone through this methodology. I promise you that the people who perform sustainably are those who implement them in their lives and businesses.

The IdeaBox™

How To Safely Manage Your Overflow
Of Ideas To Protect Your Focus

The first thing to protect yourself from is yourself—specifically your entrepreneurial brain. As entrepreneurs, our brains are one of our main assets but can become a major liability if not harnessed... If your brain is anything like mine, it is coming up with new ideas at a pace that most people wouldn't even imagine possible.

Of course, your natural instinct wants you to capitalize on these precious moments of inspiration, and you end up taking action on these immediately... I know because I used to be just like that, too. But, over time, I realized that very few of these sparks of inspiration translated into viable projects.

And while that's easy to see once you've already gone all-out and reached a dead end with an idea, it is a very costly way to try and tell apart the good from the bad ones. You simply cannot take action on each and every one of your ideas sustainably without drifting.

What's the solution? You need to find a place where you can gather all the ideas that pop in your mind during the day and then forget about them for a little while. This is going to be your IdeaBox. I came up with the IdeaBox system early on in my entrepreneurial journey. At the time, I had so many ideas that I was struggling to stay focused on my goals. It's been a fantastic way for me to manage my overly creative brain and handle idea overflow.

► Taming the Hamster and the Squirrel

Two little critters live inside our heads, feeding off our entrepreneurial juices and regulating our mental energy and our attention: the hamster and the squirrel.

The Hamster

This is something many entrepreneurs have in common: the hamster between our ears doesn't stop easily. The more you feed him, the faster he'll go.

Personally, I was always sidetracked by the multitude of ideas that were constantly going through my head. I'd ask myself, "Why can't I just focus on one thing?" but the hamster just wouldn't quit. It was always running after new ideas.

Squirrel!

You've heard about the Shiny Object Syndrome. It's ubiquitous among entrepreneurs and describes a tendency to chase after shiny new ideas, tools, or techniques instead of keeping our attention on the task or project at hand. Someone with Shiny Object Syndrome usually ends up with a long list of plans and goals, but they never get anything done. It's a disease of distraction.

If you've ever seen the Disney movie "Up," you've seen Shiny Object Syndrome in action. When Dug the dog introduces himself to Carl and Russell, he suddenly shouts, "Squirrel!" in the middle of their conversation. We all tend to do the same thing; it only takes a second for a squirrel to steal our attention and drag us off course.

The squirrel loves teasing the hamster with new objects. And the curious and fearless hamster will always want to run fast after it, eager to get its paws on a shiny new object.

You have an idea and want to act on it right away. The squirrel and the hamster are relentlessly keeping you out of focus, scattering your attention, and draining your energy. These two critters are not going to die. They are here to stay forever, and the best way to deal with them is to tame them.

The IdeaBox will help you tame them and preserve your precious focus.

It will also let you understand how your brain operates as an entrepreneur. It's a good self-awareness tool that will make you realize how you process ideas. It's also going to help you realize that not all your ideas are great, showing you that we don't always have the best natural ability when it comes to selecting good ideas. The IdeaBox is created to filter your ideas and evaluate their quality.

▶ How To Use The IdeaBox

The IdeaBox is a safe storage place for your ideas. It keeps them locked away until it's time to do, delete, or defer them.

Here's how to use it:

1. Collect your ideas in the daily IdeaBox

In the Effic Planner, there's an IdeaBox on every page.

When you have ideas that have nothing to do with your daily plans, such as your Rocks, your Routines, and other tasks you want to do that day, they need to go somewhere. The IdeaBox is that place.

You'll notice that the box is small. We've kept it this way on purpose because we want you to filter these ideas earlier rather than later. Because the space is limited, you'll have to think twice before you put an idea on paper.

At first, you'll notice that you'll tend to fill this small box all the time. You're going to think that all your ideas belong in the box.

As you learn to tame the hamster and the squirrel, you'll notice that the IdeaBox is getting less and less crowded every day. It's a sign that you've learned to curate your ideas a lot faster.

Not all your ideas are worth keeping. You have to understand your patterns when it comes to generating ideas or seeing something that you think you should act on instantly.

The IdeaBox eliminates that "insta-acting" tendency—that desire to act on an idea as fast as possible. Every time you have a new idea, whether it's for a product, for marketing, or something else, put it in the box. It's a safe place.

2. Pass your daily ideas through the 3D Filter

At the end of the day, you're going to use what we call the 3D Filter. You're going to do one of the following for each task: Do, Delete, or Defer.

If you have a great idea that could be implemented quickly, put it in your Planner as a secondary task for the next couple of days or the next week, if you have the space available.

If you're a big thinker like me, your ideas will be on a large scale. For example, you might have an idea about a new product or even a new business. These ideas require a lot more time, energy, and attention.

When this happens, you have two options. The first option is to delete the idea. I might realize that it's unrealistic and can never happen. Sometimes, as the day has gone on, I realize that an idea isn't as good as I first thought. For example, an idea I thought was good at 10 A.M. may not seem so great at 4.30 P.M. It happens a lot. Seriously.

It's like when you go to the cashier at the grocery store, you see delicious chocolate bars, and all you want to do is eat one. So you buy a bar. But when you get out of the store, you realize that it was an impulse buy, and you don't need to eat it. The same thing happens with a lot of your ideas. We entrepreneurs have this problem because it's how our brains operate. You can try to fight it. Alternatively, you can deal with it, and that's where the IdeaBox and the 3D Filter come in.

If you don't want to delete an idea entirely, you can defer it to what we call the Master IdeaBox. It's at the end of your Planner. You can create an external version, such as a spreadsheet. However, I like to put my ideas on paper. I categorize all my ideas, creating a category for marketing, for new products, for content, and so on.

IDEA **BOX**

CATEGORY: ....

- [ ] ....
- [ ] ....
- [ ] ....
- [ ] ....
- [ ] ....
- [ ] ....
- [ ] ....
- [ ] ....
- [ ] ....
- [ ] ....
- [ ] ....
- [ ] ....
- [ ] ....
- [ ] ....
- [ ] ....
- [ ] ....
- [ ] ....
- [ ] ....

3. At the end of each quarter, review the Master IdeaBox and use the 3D filter again

Look at each idea and decide whether you're going to do, delete, or defer it.

If you decide to follow through on an idea, it usually needs to become part of a Bucket. If you have it in the Master IdeaBox, that generally means it's too big to be a daily secondary task. It needs to become part of your planned workload. This doesn't mean you need to add more to your existing commitments; it means the idea becomes a priority for the next quarter. You can either make it into a new Bucket or have it be part of another Bucket.

Alternatively, you may choose to delete the idea. An idea that seemed fantastic at the beginning of the quarter might have worked back then, but may not seem so good anymore. That's common.

Finally, the third option is to defer the idea. If an idea is still good, but you don't have the capacity or space in your schedule to act on it, transfer it to the Idea Vault.

4. Place all remaining ideas in the Idea Vault

The Idea Vault is a safe place to store ideas that are not urgent but could be useful in the future. I personally have a Google Spreadsheet that does the job.

To be honest, 99% of the time, I don't ever touch the ideas in the Vault again. Because of the way I operate, I know where I'm heading a year in advance. Unless an idea is extremely good and a game-changer, I'm not going to be diverging from my planned course.

After many years of using the IdeaBox system, my brain has learned to automatically filter my ideas. I'm less distracted, and my IdeaBox gets smaller and smaller and contains fewer items. My brain has learned to filter out distracting ideas.

It's important for you to have an IdeaBox. It's a powerful tool that you'll learn to use over time. It will condition your brain to be more selective when filtering ideas. Over time, your list of ideas will get shorter. Even the Master IdeaBox is going to get emptier. A few years ago, my Master IdeaBox was always full. Now, I have a lot of space left in it at the end of every quarter. It's a beautiful thing. Use it and enjoy the process of curating ideas. If you are always tempted by new ideas, it's an awesome thing to have in your toolbox.

Toolbox:

> Download the **IdeaBox** templates and **IdeaVault** spreadsheet at *www.DoneByNoonBook.com/Toolbox*

Business Detox™
Rest & Recovery Cycles For
Burnout-Free Performance

Today's entrepreneurial culture is all about hustle and sacrifice. People don't talk about taking time off, even though it's so crucial to success. Taking time off lets you engage in reflection and deep thinking. It allows you to rest and recover, which is key for sustainable performance and your overall well-being.

The Business Detox is one of the most important things you can do as a business owner. We've already talked about the principles I've taken from the world of sports performance and how I've applied them to business. Rest and recovery is one of them. It tends to be underrated. We assume that the more we work, the better our results. But this isn't true.

Every part of the Business Detox is intimately related to how we approach Protection as a whole. It relates closely to how we approach our habits, rituals, and routines. Entrepreneurs often don't realize that they are burning out until they become completely overwhelmed. They don't usually do a very good job of preventing it.

The Business Detox helps you reset yourself physically, mentally, and emotionally at different levels. Rest and recovery will improve your health, productivity, and performance.

No matter what level you're operating at, the key is to gain some altitude. Picture yourself on an airplane. When you're on the ground, that's all you can see. It's impossible to see anything higher. However, when you take off and start gaining altitude, your view becomes broader. You can see what's really happening because you can see the bigger picture.

When we talked about the Principle of Adaptation, I showed you how to follow macro, meso, and micro cycles as you increase your workload over time. Now I'm going to show you how to do the same thing in the context of recovery.

Macro Business Detox

These cycles last 90 days. At the end of each cycle, take a week off from your business, step back, and gain some altitude.

For example, Bill Gates takes several "think weeks" per year. He locks himself away in a wooden cabin in a remote area. It gives him a chance to see things from a new perspective. He doesn't have to worry about day to day tasks. It's an opportunity for him to reevaluate things, tackle big problems, and come up with better solutions.

A "think week" gives you a valuable opportunity to do some deep thinking. Deep thinking is vigorous, critical, and life-changing. It involves questioning your assumptions and challenging your views about yourself, other people, and the world. It means focusing your attention on an idea, theory, or event and coming up with new insights instead of remaining in a state of reactivity. Deep thinking improves your creativity because it encourages you to see problems from new angles.

It also gives you a huge advantage as an entrepreneur because when you become a better thinker, your actions will have more meaning and impact. When you think deeply about yourself and your actions, you'll also uncover your dreams and values. This can be inspiring and keep you on the right track to reach goals that have meaning for you. A great benefit of following 90-day macrocycles is that you can work for 12 weeks and then take the 13th week off. It's fully integrated into your quarter.

It can be hard to take breaks when you're a busy entrepreneur, so I recommend you block them off in your calendar and work around them. Try to plan your Macro Business Detoxes a year in advance.

I'm warning you now: At first, you will feel massive resistance towards the idea. You're probably telling yourself, "Oh, I can't just take off a full week." But when you make your structure better and protect it, taking this time off will just become part of how you operate. A lot of people think that because they are so busy in the present, the moment they stop, their business will grind to a halt. When you implement the Effic methodology, you'll free up a lot more time. This will allow you to build the systems you need to create a business that can thrive even when you're not there. The quality of these week-long Macro Detoxes will be highly dependent on how evolved your structure is. In the first year, you might not take time off every 12 weeks. However, you might do it twice, and that's fine. The more progress you make, and the more processes you build, the easier it will be to take those breaks. It will be difficult, but please schedule them. You could start smaller, perhaps with two or three-day vacations. Just start somewhere.

If you have kids, it might be difficult to make that week off a "think week." You'll more than often use that week to spend time with the family. However, Karine and I always schedule some deep thinking time during these Macro Detoxes. We pro-actively plan full days where we can be alone individually and at least one just the two of us to evaluate alignment together. Even if you're not alone for most of that week, remember that the main goal here is for you to disconnect from the business and gain altitude.

We all need time to gain altitude and reevaluate. Use that week-long break to think carefully about your next 90 days. Even if you have a good idea of where you're heading, it's always great to sit back with your Planner and put it down on paper. Take the time and review where you're at. More often than not, this will allow you to think at a different level because you're not deep in day to day tasks.

It's a perfect time to look at your Annual Guideline and amend it if needed. Look at what will be in your Buckets for the next quarter and plan ahead. Think of it this way: If you have a car, you need to change your oil and align its wheels regularly to make sure it runs properly and will work well for a long time. It's the same with your Annual Guideline; evaluating it is like an alignment check for your business. I recommend re-writing your Big Picture every year, during the last Macro Business Detox. It's a fantastic way to build self and business awareness.

Meso Business Detox

Each mesocycle is one week long. I recommend you have two full days off per week, preferably consecutive.

Personally, I take my weekends off. I work Monday to Friday, which sounds very traditional, but I've realized that if I want to perform at my best and be a great Dad, husband, and friend, I need a more traditional structure. Because most entrepreneurs go into business for freedom, they will resist structure. It's a big mistake, especially if you have a family.

When it was just me and my wife, we'd take random time off. We didn't even care what day of the week it was. Then, when the kids arrived, we needed more structure.

Now, I close my laptop on Friday afternoons and don't open it until Monday morning. It's non-negotiable. Over the weekend, I spend time with my family, socialize, and do non-work activities. As a result, I always start the next week feeling refreshed. I come back and cannot wait to work on Monday because I know I'm going to have an exciting week. I know exactly what I'm going to be doing.

Taking two consecutive days off allows your brain to take a short but long enough break from making the day to day decisions that are part of running a business, giving you more energy to devote to your business. Giving yourself enough time away from your work will help you make better, more analytical decisions when you return. Try to unplug from your devices as well, or at least keep them out of your pocket. Making time to participate in your hobbies and to socialize with family and friends without having to think about work keeps you well-rounded and mentally healthy.

Keep in mind that the effectiveness of your structure will be dependent on its level of optimization. In fact, just like your Macro Detoxes are closely connected to your 90-day planning, Meso Detoxes rely on the successful implementation of your Done By Noon schedule.

You don't need to imitate my schedule. You don't have to take two days off per week immediately or stop working on weekends. But not working towards it would be a mistake. Think strategically. It's like working out. If you exercise intensely for seven days per week, you'll stop seeing it because your body needs time to recover. You'll be growing when you rest, and it's the same in business.

Micro Business Detox

This is your daily detox cycle.

As you know now, your schedule contains different types of tasks, each with their own energetic costs. The Done By Noon framework takes this into account and empowers you to optimize your daily work performance. It also forces you to schedule personal activities, which helps you achieve a healthier work-life harmony.

However, these strategies alone won't guarantee that you get enough daily Rest and Recovery. You must also learn how to move between Work Mode and Human Mode. To do this, you need two things: a set of daily self-care practices, and a transition ritual between work time and personal time. The goal here is not to have work and life compete against each other. Work isn't the enemy. The real enemy is a poor self-leadership style that results in a life dedicated solely to work. Instead, we want to enhance your discipline by eliminating negative habits and replacing them with sustainably integrated high-performance ones for your life and business.

That's why we have created an easy to implement Self-Care and Evening Checkout processes. If you don't discipline yourself to go through these daily, you can't expect to perform sustainably, have good work-life harmony, and be fully present with yourself or your family. Self-Discipline is one of the pillars of good Self-Leadership. This is what we'll show you how to implement next.

Daily Self-Care

The 5-Step Daily Routine To
Keep Your Physical, Mental &
Emotional Health In Check

As Peter Drucker said, "In business, you cannot manage other people unless you manage yourself first."

We've already talked about the importance of self-leadership in business, and it starts with self-care. You need to take care of yourself in a way that is going to allow you to perform at your best.

We've created a five-step daily self-care routine for you to follow, and we've integrated it into the Effic Planner. This is why the Effic methodology is so popular—we put human beings at the center of what we do. We understand that your business performance, sustainable entrepreneurial success, and productivity starts with you.

These five steps might or might not be part of your morning routine. It depends on how you structure your day and your context. For example, you might perform it as a one-hour sequence at the beginning of every day. If you're like me and have kids, it's tough to do it in a single shot in the morning, so

I spread my routine throughout the day. Before I had kids, I was able to do all my self-care in the morning, but now I have to divide it up.

What's important is that your self-care routine becomes part of how you lead yourself through the day. The key is to build self-discipline, which in turn helps you create long-lasting habits. When I was seriously involved in fitness and sports performance, a lot of the habits I implemented in my life helped me acquire discipline that I could bring to my entrepreneurial journey. For example, I ate food at a specific time, exercised in a certain way, and went to bed at a particular time. This self-discipline was a huge advantage for me in business.

Your Effic Planner outlines the building blocks we recommend you use as the basics of your self-care routine. You can expand on it as much as you want. The key is to find the right self-care recipe that works for you. It's like physical training. No single routine will work for everyone. However, the basics apply to everyone. If they are in place, everything will be fine, and that's the case here when it comes to self-care.

Here's your 5-step daily care routine:

Step 1: Hydration

Up to 80% of adults are chronically dehydrated. It's higher in hot countries, like Australia, but it's not much better in the United States (75%) or Canada (70%). So this means that most of us walk around in a state of dehydration. It can cause fatigue, brain fog, and a drop in metabolism. Although it sounds simple, drinking water has a tremendous effect on your overall well-being, performance, productivity, and even success. There's a good reason it's the first item on this list.

What I recommend is a simple habit that I've integrated into my mornings for the past 15 years. I begin each day with a tall glass of water. Every morning, I pour myself a 500 ml glass and drink it all right away. This rehydrates me after a night of sleep and ensures I am properly hydrated when I start my day. After I've finished my glass, I fill up a two-liter jug with water. I have a metal jug that I carry with me everywhere. At the end of my day, I make sure it's completely empty. This means I always have at least 2.5 L of water per day. More often than not, I have even more.

That first glass of water doesn't just hydrate me. It also acts as an activation trigger. My day hasn't really started until I've had it. Over the years, it's become a trigger that means my morning routine or self-care routine has begun.

It sounds very simple, but you have no idea how many people don't drink water. They'll tell you that they don't like it because it "doesn't taste like anything." I understand that. Often, they are addicted to other drinks, like diet drinks or coffee. But there are so many ways to make it more enjoyable. For example, you can add a few lemon slices. When we talk about hydration, we're talking about the very basics of self-care. You can go without food for a long time, but only a few days without water. If you don't drink it, you die. It's essential.

Step 2: Exercise

Studies show that a lack of exercise can be as deadly as smoking. Unfortunately, exercise is one of the first things to go out the window when you get busy in business because you always have so many other things to do. This takes a toll on your health.

Many modern-day entrepreneurs live mostly sedentary lifestyles, at a desk working on a computer at a specific place, so they don't move around as much as they should. You need to incorporate exercise into your daily life.

You can have a specific exercise plan, but you don't have to. The goal is simply to sweat every day. Beyond the physical benefits, exercise also has lots of mental health benefits. You'll be less stressed, you'll sleep better, you'll have more confidence, and you'll have more energy. Physical training contributes to mental health in so many ways.

You might have noticed that even if you dread going to the gym, you feel so much better after your workout. Exercise gives you mental clarity. It helps you feel more awake. I recommend a minimum of 20 minutes per day.

It could be walking, running, yoga, going to the gym, or any type of sport. Personally, I now go to the gym three times a week and play hockey twice a week. On the weekend, I take walks with my family or do other outdoor activities. It doesn't need to be complicated, just make a commitment to sweat every day!

Step 3: Gratitude

As an athlete and as a man, gratitude is something I overlooked for many years. It wasn't until I faced major adversity in a challenging period of my personal and professional life where I was on the verge of burnout that I started incorporating it daily in my life.

At that time, life and business had thrown a series of curveballs my way in a short period of time. I was completely mentally and emotionally burned out. I felt like I was caught in the eye of a hurricane and couldn't see through it.

I sought counsel from one of my great friends who had faced many big challenges in his life as an entrepreneur. I asked him how I should go about getting out of the turmoil I was caught in. I expected a long and elaborate answer along with a plan. Instead, he said this: "Gratitude. Gratitude really saved me from dark times. You need to start practicing it daily."

This statement seemed too simple, yet it ended up being one of the most powerful and life-changing pieces of advice I ever received.

I started being grateful for small things every day. Things like having drinkable water on demand, access to the internet, eyesight, or even electricity. I saw results right away. My anxiety started going away, and it helped me release a lot of toxic emotions.

When it's chaos, it's easy to focus on the negative things in life. When we keep thinking like this, our brains start to see life through a darker lens. Deliberately practicing gratitude trains your brain to think positively.

There are tools you can use to do this, including gratitude journals, but I don't like to spend a lot of time writing long lists of gratitudes. It can get redundant. To help myself and my clients, I came up with a simple technique called the Reconnection Phrase:

"Today, I am grateful for_____,
and I keep in mind that_____."

The phrase starts, "Today, I am grateful for…" and you need to fill in the blank with one thing you are grateful for.

It's so easy to lose sight of what we have, especially in the modern world. We don't even realize what we've got. My wife Karine is a psychotherapist, and her clients tend to look on the darker side of life. One thing she always tells them to start with is to be grateful for their hands and to imagine how much harder life would be without them. It's obvious, and it's true. If you have two hands, consider yourself privileged. It's a miracle that we have two hands with five fingers each that allow us to do so many things. We take them for granted, as we do with so many other things. It's so important to remind ourselves every day of one thing.

I'm like everyone else. Sometimes I run out of things to say, so I revert back to the two hands example. Gratitude rewires my brain daily. It shows me a new way to see things, even if it's just for that day. It helps me stay in a very positive mindset and to focus on the things that are important.

The second part of the reconnection phrase is, "And I keep in mind that…" This part is to help you keep in mind something important for you. Something that you need to keep alive in your consciousness. You could write that you will prioritize your self-care daily, that you want to have a particular impact in the world, or that you want to accomplish something specific. It could also be something entirely personal; it doesn't matter as long as you keep in mind what drives you.

Be grateful for what you have. When you have nothing, you revert back to being thankful for the most basic things. But you don't have to wait until you've got nothing. We live in a world of abundance. We're privileged, and losing sight of that is crazy. Reconnect daily by cultivating gratitude and keeping your true motivation in sight.

Step 4: Meditation

There are many benefits to meditation. It improves your brain fitness and helps you perform better. It's a fantastic thing to do. However, if you're like me, you might not be a fan of sitting down for an extended period of time in the lotus position while saying, "Ommm," which is what a lot of people imagine when they hear the word "meditation." That was my perception for a long time.

Then I discovered that meditation can be whatever you want it to be. Meditation is just about training your brain to center and focus, and redirect your thoughts. It's a powerful self-awareness tool.

So, there's no magic recipe, but there are three basic parts: environment, breathing, and mindfulness.

Here's my personal recipe. I spend 5-15 minutes by myself. It's not easy now that I'm married and have children because it's not very often that I'm alone, but I always find time for it. I have a very nice sunroom I can use in the winter when it's cold. In the summer, I go out on the patio outside. I'm grateful and thankful that I live in front of a beautiful river. I sit down and watch it flow by.

As I sit, I breathe deeply, inhaling and exhaling. I focus on that breathing. It takes my mind off any stupid thoughts I might have or things in my brain that are clogging my vision or taking up my attention. Thoughts will start entering my head. I just acknowledge them without taking action. They come, and they go. I become mindful and aware of these thoughts and aware of the fact I live in the present moment. You have to experience it for yourself to understand.

Doing this every day has been a game-changer for my focus and well-being. It's also helped my productivity because I feel refreshed every single day. So, meditation doesn't need to be a long, complicated process. I think so many people who teach meditation techniques are at such an advanced level that they forget that it's intimidating for a lot of us.

I've never been a big fan of long or structured meditation; it's just not my style. But I use these three basic ingredients, and it works. If you're more advanced when it comes to meditation, that's great, just keep practicing daily.

Step 5: Healthy Eating

This is a no-brainer. Food and water impact every aspect of your health, not just from a physical standpoint. What you eat and drink will also affect your emotional and mental state. These days, there are so many types of diets and ways of eating, from keto diets to veganism.

I'm not here to tell you that one is better than the other. As someone who has been in the fitness game for a long time, I've used some extreme diets for muscle growth and fat loss. You can trust me when I tell you these diets are not sustainable. Having moved beyond them, I think the most sustainable approach is to focus on eating for energy.

To perform sustainably for a long time, you need to focus on digestion. I never really paid attention to digestion until I became a partner at BiOptimizers. BiOptimizers manufactures digestive supplements such as enzymes and probiotics.

I realized that digestion takes a humongous amount of energy, and we don't even know it. Think about how you feel after a big meal. You feel sluggish, sleepy, and tired. That's because your body is working hard to digest the food you've just eaten.

Our digestion changes over time. If you're in your 20's, you probably don't have any digestion problems. That will change as you get older. Now that I'm older, I have problems digesting certain foods. It's not that they make me sick; they just make me feel a lot less energetic.

Grains are one example. I used to be the biggest fan of oatmeal and would eat it every morning. But gradually, I realized that I wasn't digesting it as well as I used to.

You can take blood tests to figure out what's going on. They will tell you what you should eat and what to avoid, so they're a good investment. You should listen to your body, but you should also be aware that science can now help us out.

Personally, I have to be careful about eating some types of foods. I use a range of dieting strategies, including fasting. It's not for everyone, but I'm a big fan and fast at least once per week. I also include probiotics and enzymes in my diet to help me digest food better. It helps with my energy levels and productivity.

The older you get, the more you understand the importance of digestion and energy. We don't think about it until our backs are against the wall. At that point, we start to think, "Well, now it's time to be a little bit more intentional about it."

When it comes to healthy eating, the key is to be prepared. Managing your diet is like managing work. If you are reactive to your environment, you're going to make bad decisions. When you're not prepared with your food, you're going to revert to things that are fast and easy to make. Unfortunately, these are not always the healthiest options. Having plans and routines will help you make intentional choices.

I'm not going to tell you to follow a particular diet. We're all different. Focus on learning what helps you maintain a good level of energy. Nutrition is a very deep topic, but if you stick to the basics, you'll be fine.

As a whole, this five-step routine contains the basics for great physical, mental, and emotional health. If you follow it, you'll have most of your self-care covered.

Your Sleep

Although I didn't officially include it in the self-care routine since it's a mandatory daily life function, you should also take a deep look at your sleep. If you don't get enough, your health and productivity will suffer. When you're asleep, every organ and system in your body gets a much-needed chance to recuperate. This includes your brain. It needs adequate rest to perform at its best.

According to a study carried out by the National Sleep Foundation, adults need a minimum of 7 hours of sleep per night. Your sleeping patterns will change as you move through life. This is particularly true if you have kids. If you're a parent, it might be a long time since you had a good night's sleep.

A lack of sleep causes serious side-effects. In one study, 48 healthy adults aged between 21 and 38 were split into four groups. Three of the groups were allowed to sleep for either 4, 6, or 8 hours per night for 14 days. The last group went entirely without sleep for up to 3 days.

The researchers compared each group's performance on a range of cognitive tasks. They found that the less sleep the participants got, the worse their performance. Sleeping for 6 hours or 4 hours per night took an increasing toll on the participants as the days passed. After ten days, the participants who were only sleeping 6 hours per night were getting similar test scores to people who had been totally deprived of sleep for two days. Going without sleep for a single night has such a detrimental effect on your thinking ability that, from your brain's point of view, you may as well be drunk.

You might think that you can make up for lost sleep with a couple of long nights or a lie-in. Sleep doesn't work that way. In the study, participants were given a chance to sleep as much as they wanted for three nights at the end of the experiment. When they were tested again, it was clear their thinking abilities hadn't yet returned to normal. You can't skimp on sleep during the week and then try to make up for it on the weekend.

To make matters worse, we're often unaware that we're short on sleep. In the study, the participants who only got 6 hours per night often said they felt fine, even though their test scores showed otherwise. Self-awareness and self-honesty are important here. There are no shortcuts. Consistency is key. Seven to 8 hours of sleep should be your goal.

What changed it for me was to set a maximum bedtime each day at 10:00 P.M. Some days, when I feel a bit more tired I go to bed a bit earlier, but never later than 10:00 P.M. This allows me to wake up early knowing I consistently get a minimum of 7 hours of sleep per day. It wasn't easy as I always considered myself an evening person. I used to always go to bed around midnight. When my first daughter was born, I realized I was playing Russian roulette by doing so. The value of my sleep immediately went up drastically, and I had to make the proper adjustments even though I liked being up late. Sometimes, the best way to initiate change is to give yourself no other choice when your back is against the wall. I did, and I'm happy about it because I'm now collecting the dividends.

The Evening Checkout™
The Simple Ritual To Effectively Transition
Between Work Time And Personal Time

Let me ask you a question: what do you do before you check out of a hotel room? Most of the time, it goes like this: you look around, check that you haven't forgotten anything, pick up your bags, take your keys, exit the room, and then bring the keys to the front desk. After you hand over the keys, you can't enter your room again. It's done, your stay is over, and you've successfully checked out.

You should do the same thing in your business in order to transition between work time and family time. To help you do that, we've created a process you should use at the end of every workday: the Evening Checkout.

Based on your schedule, you need to establish a daily checkout time. The time will depend on your context and when you want your workday to be over. For me, it's never later than 5:00 P.M. Most days it's earlier.

The Evening Checkout routine shouldn't take more than 5-10 minutes.

Just like the Self-Care routine, it has five steps:

Step 1: Get Out Of Your Inbox

When you use the Done By Noon framework, you should allow a specific time for emails in one of your FocusBoxes. We've developed a great system—the Inbox Freedom System—that you can grab for free at inboxfreedomsystem.com. This is the exact system I used to go from having hundreds of emails daily to achieve inbox zero every day by the time I check out. It's extremely powerful.

After completing the checkout process, you should stay out of your inbox for the rest of the day. Constantly checking emails is a distracting habit you need to break. Some people check their emails an insanely high number of times each day, and it undermines their focus and productivity.

Worried about emergencies? Don't worry about it. We'll show you how to eliminate them using the Inbox Freedom System. As a bonus, we'll even show you how to turn your inbox into an automated sales generating tool.

Step 2: Purge The IdeaBox

Apply the 3D Filter—do, delete, or defer—for each task. If you decide to do the task, add it to the list of secondary reactive tasks you have for that week if you have space. Delete it if it's irrelevant. Defer it to the Master IdeaBox if it fits in a Bucket and you want to tackle it in an upcoming quarter.

Step 3: Purge Your Notes

The Notes space on the right side of your Planner is a free space. You can use it however you like. Many people write their ideas or important information on Post-It notes, which end up scattered around their offices. There's a high chance that these notes are never acted upon.

At the end of the day, I either transfer my notes to my secondary task list for the rest of the week if I have enough space, or I put them on FIONA's desk to be processed the following Monday. I don't have any loose notes. The problem with loose notes is that, even if you don't realize it, they are a distraction because they are always in the back of your mind.

Step 4: Turn Off Your Phone

This will be hard, but I'm going to challenge you to turn off your phone.

Increasingly, we're getting addicted to our phones. The problem with smartphones is that they are an open line that makes us available to everyone 24/7. It's like leaving the door of your house open at all times. Would you want people to be able to come and go whenever they want? Probably not. It's the same thing with your phone. Unless you draw some boundaries, people can and will contact you whenever they want.

People find it hard to tell whether something is truly urgent or whether it can wait. They don't have a filter. As I explained when I talked about the Eisenhower Matrix, many people don't understand whether something is an emergency or not unless you create some clear guidelines.

Turning off your phone will eliminate reactivity and false emergencies. If you use the Inbox Freedom System, I'll ask you to activate an inbox responder. You can do the same thing with your phone. If people call or text, you can send automated replies or have a voicemail that says, "If it's truly a life or death emergency, here's another way you can reach me." Personally, I direct people to my home phone number for real emergencies. If it's absolutely necessary, they can contact me there. If something is truly urgent, they will find a way to reach me.

I think we tend to anxiously worry about what could happen, but the odds of something very important and urgent happening are extremely low. Guess how many calls I've received over the past five years? None. Why? Because there have been no real emergencies. We have fireproofed our business using the Effic method so that I don't have to worry that if something bad happens, someone won't be able to reach me.

It will also allow you to be more present. If you have a family, you need to realize that no one likes to have dinner with someone who is on their phone answering emails. To create and maintain harmony in your life and business, keep it turned off after your checkout.

Turning off your phone will also boost your creativity. When you're constantly interrupted, your mind and thoughts are molded by notifications, emails, and social media. When you turn on your phone, you automatically refresh your favorite apps. It's second nature; you don't even think about it. You become a robot, rather than a creative human being.

Being away from your phone can leave you in a state of boredom. You won't be able to refresh your apps 16 times to make sure you aren't missing anything. You'll be forced to think about and do something else instead. Research from the field of neuroscience has shown that we use the same mental processes for daydreaming as we do for imagination and creativity. When you daydream or don't have anything to do, you'll be able to access a more creative space. Creativity is what makes us great as entrepreneurs. It's one of our biggest assets. The more creative we are, the better we become at solving problems, creating products, and offering solutions to people. So, the more creative we are, the better we perform. That's why I invite you to only turn it back on when you open your Communication FocusBox.

Just like the Business Detox, you might feel a lot of resistance at the thought of turning off your phone, but if you include it as part of your checkout ritual and make it a habit, it's powerful.

Step 5: Make Tomorrow's List Of Tasks

Plan your Small Rocks, Secondary Tasks, and Routines for the next day. Make sure you're aware of any upcoming meetings or calls. When you start work again the following morning, you'll know exactly what you have to do without having to think about it. You'll bypass a lot of stress and will be able to get straight to work. If you wait until the next day to figure out what you're going to do, you leave the door open to distractions. By making your list the day before and scheduling any outstanding tasks, you'll be able to stay focused.

Once you've checked all the Evening Checkout boxes, you don't have to worry about anything. Your inbox is under control, your ideas are recorded, your notes are sorted out, your phone won't wake you up in the middle of the night, and your tasks for the next day are locked and loaded. All you have to do is close your Effic Planner for the day, and you're fully checked out.

The Evening Checkout is the final part of Protection, which shields your structure, time, energy, and attention. Through these tools and sets of routines, rituals, and habits, you'll achieve the protection you need to preserve a high-performance structure and maintain sustainable harmony between your life and your business.

Putting It All Together

Your First 90 Days

I promised you this wasn't a quick fix or a senseless collection of hacks. You have here a method that will allow you to perform sustainably while ensuring you're always focusing on your top personal and professional priorities.

Before you start taking action daily, let's quickly sum up the steps we've looked at so far. These are the steps that you need to have covered before you start integrating the Effic Method into your entrepreneurial life.

Step 1: You **Projected** yourself into the future. You now have a clear **Big Picture,** and you've aligned it with an **Annual Guideline** made up of 5 goals you want to see become a reality within the next 12 months.

Step 2: You have established your work **Priorities** by filling up your Buckets with **Rocks** for the next 90 days and built a set of **Routines** that you will optimize over time using the **D.O.A. Map.**

Step 3: You have created your **Schedule** using the **Done By Noon Framework.** You have proactively __Planned__ your first week by filling your **FocusBoxes**, listing your **Small Rocks** as priority actions, making a list of your secondary tasks, and planning your **Routines** for each day.

Step 4: You are ready to actively __Protect__ your structure armed with the **IdeaBox**, your **Daily Self-Care Routine**, and your **Evening Checkout Ritual**. You have also planned your **Business Detoxes.**

You are now ready to take action daily. To support you and keep you accountable, here is a sample of the daily planning pages of the Effic Planner.

To make it easy for you, all the templates you need, including a free printable version of the daily planner and a tutorial, are available to download in the Toolbox at www.DoneByNoon-Book.com/Toolbox. If you want more information about the Effic Planner, you can visit www.EfficPlanner.com.

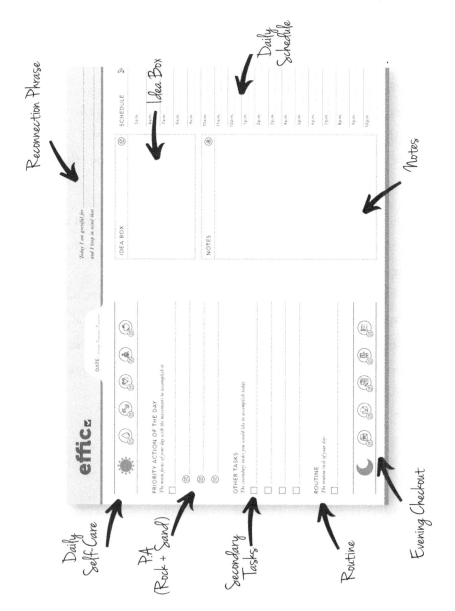

Reconnection Phrase

Today I am grateful for
and I keep in mind that

DATE: ___/___/___

effic℞

☀ PRIORITY ACTION OF THE DAY
The main focus of your day with the movements to accomplish it

OTHER TASKS
The secondary tasks you would like to accomplish today

ROUTINE
The routine task of your day

🌙

Daily Self-Care

P.A.
(Rock + Sand)

Secondary Tasks

Routine

Evening Checkout

IDEA BOX

Idea Box

NOTES

Notes

SCHEDULE

5a.m.
6a.m.
7a.m.
8a.m.
9a.m.
10a.m.
11a.m.
12p.m.
1p.m.
2p.m.
3p.m.
4p.m.
5p.m.
6p.m.
7p.m.
8p.m.
9p.m.
10p.m.

Daily Schedule

Once you have completed your first week, perform the **Weekly Review** process, and plan your next week.

WEEK 1 **REVIEW**

- Review annual guideline and quarterly buckets
- My 3 best small wins of the week:
  - ☑
  - ☑
  - ☑
- How I will celebrate them:
- My obstacles of the week:
- My weekly self-awareness scorecard:

  Energy ○○○○○ Clarity & Focus ○○○○○ Productivity ○○○○○ Satisfaction ○○○○○

- What I will improve next week:
- Revise notes
- Make next week's list

2

WEEKLY LIST

PRIORITY ACTIONS

☐ ☐ ☐ ☐ ☐ ☐ ☐ ☐

OTHER TASKS

☐ ☐ ☐ ☐ ☐ ☐ ☐ ☐

ROUTINES

☐ M ☐ F
☐ T ☐ S
☐ W ☐ S
☐ T

Commit to the process for the next 90 days. At the end of your quarter, review the past 90 days using **The Quarterly Review** process and plan your next quarter.

QUARTERLY **REVIEW**

☐ Review annual guideline and quarterly buckets

☐ My biggest win this quarter is:

....

☐ What I wasn't able to accomplish this quarter:

....

....

....

☐ Top 3 things I've learned this quarter:

☑ ....

☑ ....

☑ ....

☐ What I am committing to improve next quarter:

....

....

....

☐ Plan my next Business Detox (unplugged vacation time)

☐ Empty the idea box

☐ Get a new Effic Planner

☐ Establish buckets for next quarter

Again, don't worry if your first quarter isn't perfect. It usually takes a minimum of 2 quarters to start mastering the method.

So even if you don't feel in full control at the beginning, don't panic! It's a learning process, like starting a new sport or any other new activity.

You won't be at your best after the first session, but you will improve, and over time it will become second nature. As your Self-Leadership skills improve, you will notice that you'll be able to gauge your workload better and fill your Buckets more efficiently and effectively. You will gradually optimize and implement systems so you can operate within your zone of power more often. This will empower you to reclaim precious space in your schedule.

After a year has gone by, I invite you to go through your Big Picture exercise again to ensure that you aren't drifting. Refresh and solidify your vision of what you truly want from your entrepreneurial life. Make it an annual Routine.

If you stay committed to the process, your success is guaranteed.

Conclusion

"Live Free or Die"

I remember the first time I saw this motto on a license plate from the state of New Hampshire. Because they convey such an assertive pledge for independence, these four words left a strong impression on me.

Because freedom is really what they are after, this is a motto I'd like all entrepreneurs to live by as well. Every entrepreneur should live by their own definition of freedom and success. You might want more time freedom, others will want more financial freedom, many will want more creative freedom. Unfortunately, most entrepreneurs will let this freedom die.

The truth is, no one told you entrepreneurship would be this way. In a broken business culture that promotes workaholism and non-stop hustle, where productivity and performance are measured by quantity over quality, we are often confronted with unmanageable workloads, focus-robbing reactivity, and deep overwhelm.

The dream is gradually replaced by frustrations. You never get to work on valuable projects that will drive your business forward. You don't see the financial results you want, even though you work a lot. Worst of all, there's also the frustration of knowing that you never have enough time for what is most important to you in life.

If being your own boss is not what you had in mind when you first started, the great news is that you are in control. It's time to stop putting your own needs last and to start strategically managing your finite resources—time, energy, and attention—to become more efficient and effective.

It will require you to become a great self-leader while building the right structure and systems so you can have the space to live your entrepreneurial life the way you want.

Success is how you define it. It's your right to strive for meaning and fulfillment in your life and work, something modern humans have lost in the chaos of a fast-moving world. Whatever your personal definition of success is, keep in mind that you won't earn a medal for working frantically. Still, you'll always be recognized for the results and impact you provide, whether it's in your professional or personal life.

I believe in you.

Dave

About The Author

Dave Ruel is a former competitive physique athlete turned serial entrepreneur, author, speaker, and leadership mentor.

After founding and growing multi-million dollar online companies in the field of health, fitness, and sports nutrition for nearly a decade, Dave saw the dark side of entrepreneurship gradually rob him of his freedom, leaving him burned out and unfulfilled. Refusing to conform to a broken business culture that promotes workaholism and non-stop hustle, Dave created a sustainable structure and systems for his life and business to reclaim his freedom without sacrificing the growth of his companies.

Fueled by his passion for entrepreneurship and human performance, he launched Effic, an innovative leadership development company that helps busy entrepreneurs maximize their impact and freedom.

Following his "efficiency first" philosophy to entrepreneurial productivity and performance, Dave developed a powerful methodology that he sums up in the best-selling book *Done By Noon˚ - How To Achieve More By Noon Than Other Entrepreneurs In A Full Day.*

Effic's systems, frameworks, and tools, including the Effic Planner, are now used by thousands of entrepreneurs all around the world. Effic has also built a fast-growing network of Effic Certified Partners who teach the methodology on three continents, in countries including Australia, the United Kingdom, Norway, Canada, and the USA.

Dave lives on the East Coast of Canada with his wife Karine and their two daughters.

Additional Resources, Tools & Trainings

► Done By Noon® Book Toolbox

Access this book's free support resources at
www.DoneByNoonBook.com/Toolbox

► Done By Noon® Express Masterclass

Watch a free 15-minute accelerated video training at
www.BeDoneByNoon.com

► The Effic® Planner

Get our best-selling planner for entrepreneurs at
www.EfficPlanner.com

► Podcast

Listen to our Podcast at www.DoneByNoonPodcast.com

► For More Tools, Trainings, And Resources, Please Visit
www.Effic.co

Work With Us

How Would You Like To Earn Up To
$87 For Each Person
That Reads Done By Noon With You?

If You Liked The Book, You Can Help Your Friends And Followers Achieve Their Goals Faster And Get Paid To Do So.

How Does It Work?

It's Simple. Promote The Done By Noon Book And Earn Up To $87 For Each Book Sold!

Every time someone claims their copy of the Done By Noon Book using your unique referral link, you get paid.

Your special referral (or "affiliate") link also tracks additional purchases. So if someone buys additional products, tools, or trainings, you'll automatically earn a commission for those sales too.

It's a huge win-win for both you and your network you share this book with.

And yes - it's really that simple!

To Get Your Unique Referral Link For Done By Noon, Go To:

www.EfficAffiliates.com

Made in the USA
Monee, IL
24 January 2023

26077063R00162